SANDSTONE SPINE

Seeking the

Anasazi on

the First

Traverse

of the

Comb Ridge

SANDSTONE SPINE

DAVID ROBERTS
PHOTOGRAPHS BY GREG CHILD

THE MOUNTAINEERS BOOKS

THE MOUNTAINEERS BOOKS
is the nonprofit publishing arm of The Mountaineers Club, an organization founded in 1906 and dedicated to the exploration, preservation, and enjoyment of outdoor and wilderness areas.

1001 SW Klickitat Way, Suite 201, Seattle, WA 98134

First edition, 2006

Manufactured in the United States of America

Acquiring Editor: Cassandra Conyers
Project Editor: Laura Drury
Copy Editor: Joeth Zucco
Cover, Book Design, and Layout: Mayumi Thompson
Cartographer: Moore Creative Designs
Photographer: Greg Child

Cover photograph: *Anasazi cliff dwelling and Comb Ridge (inset)*
Back cover photograph: *Potsherd*
Frontispiece: *Chinle Wash*

Library of Congress Cataloging-in-Publication Data
Roberts, David, 1943-
  Sandstone Spine : first traverse of the Comb Ridge / David Roberts ; photographs by Greg Child.-- 1st ed.
      p. cm.
  Includes bibliographical references and index.
  ISBN 1-59485-004-6 (pbk. : alk. paper) -- ISBN 1-59485-005-4 (hardcover : alk. paper)
 1. Backpacking--Utah-Comb Ridge, Navajo Reservation. 2. Pueblo Indians--Antiquities. 3. Comb Ridge (Utah) I. Title.
  GV199.44.U8R63 2005
  917.92'59--dc22
                                        2005029007

CONTENTS

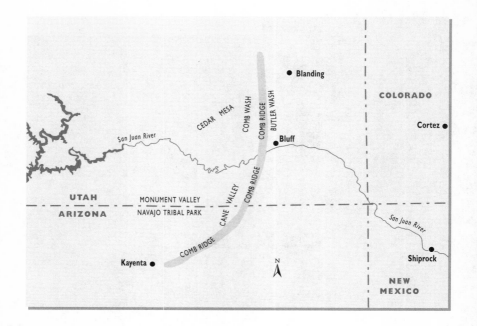

Author's Note: In this book, I have chosen sometimes to be deliberately vague about the name and location of certain prehistoric ruins and rock art. Such an ethic is by now in long use among writers, photographers, and guides who celebrate the Southwest. A narrative of personal discovery should not serve as a treasure map. The dogged sleuth can find just about any ancient site reported in the literature—but let her do her own homework.

During the last ten years, there has been a movement afoot to abolish the use of the term "Anasazi." The argument is that the appellation, a Navajo word meaning roughly "ancient enemies," is offensive to the Puebloans who are the descendants of the so-called Anasazi. The proposed substitute is "Ancestral Puebloans," and that designation has increasingly cropped up in the archaeological literature and the popular media.

Yet quite aside from being an awkward mouthful, "Ancestral Puebloans" imports problems of its own—"Puebloan," meaning simply "town dweller," being another name given the indigenes by an enemy, in this case the Spanish conquistadors. In recent years, a growing number of archaeologists and writers have resisted the politically-correct tide and gone back to using the term Anasazi. Since its introduction

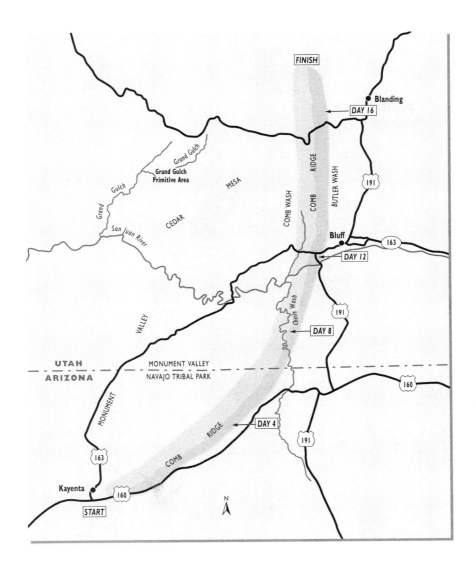

in 1936, the term, as strictly applied to a prehistoric people who flourished across the Southwest before the Spanish *entrada* of 1540, has been
extremely useful, in distinguishing that culture, for instance, from such
contemporary neighbors as the Mogollon, Hohokam, and Fremont.
And in a new book, *Painted by a Distant Hand*, Harvard's Steven
A. LeBlanc, one of the country's leading Southwesternists, argues aggressively that Anasazi has long been mistranslated. What the term

really means, LeBlanc maintains, is "ancient others"—"that is, people who were not Navajo and who preceded the Navajos—an accurate description of reality."

In this book, I follow the practice of LeBlanc and others, employing Anasazi throughout, in preference to Ancestral Puebloans.

DRY RUN

LESS THAN TWO HOURS INTO OUR first day on Comb Ridge, we made the first of many discoveries the long journey would bestow upon us. From a sand dune on its northwest side, we had scrambled up slanting ramps to the crest of the sharp escarpment. There we had dropped our heavy packs and set out on a half-day loop toward the south, where we explored three parallel fingers of rimrock separated by three abrupt mini-canyons. As we traversed the second gorge, we looked up to be startled by a perfect natural arch framing the sky only a hundred feet above us.

Those hundred feet were too steep and smooth to climb, however. There's something about an arch that teases you with the urge to clamber through it: you want to be the needle sewing that stitch in the slickrock. So we circled around to the north and tried to approach the arch from above. Once more we were stymied, this time by a satellite arch, a small trapdoor laid horizontally above the bigger arch, like a skylight in an atrium. We could scramble down into an eerie hollow that spilled toward the trapdoor but dared not push through that skylight into the void below.

While Greg and Vaughn probed the double arch's defenses, I

retreated, for something had caught my eye. Sure enough, the sandy shelf above the hollow was strewn with brightly colored potsherds. I picked up the prettier ones, fingered them lovingly, and then dropped them back in the sand. *What were the Old Ones doing here?* I wondered. *What did the double arch mean to them?*

Now we crossed the second rimrock finger, angling toward the third defile, a short box canyon running south out of the Comb. Vaughn saw it first. "Look at that, guys," he said softly.

Camouflaged by morning shadows, huddled inside a natural alcove on the far side of the gorge and facing west, stood the ruins of a small prehistoric village. We got out our binoculars, sat down, and probed the forgotten town. Then we scooted down the slab before us, crossed the dry wash in the bottom of the canyon, and diagonaled up a matching slab into the ruin.

We spent the next hour in a rapture of close attention. I counted ten rooms in the site as well as one of those round underground chambers archaeologists call a kiva. Each room was built of carefully shaped sandstone blocks mortared together with mud. The most striking edifice, as well as the most bizarre, was a two-story curvilinear building that dominated the right-hand end of the ruin—a tower of some sort, with small windows.

From its style, we knew the village had been erected in the twelfth or thirteenth century AD. It was the work of the Anasazi, ancestors of today's Pueblo Indians who occupy some twenty insular towns ranging from Taos in northern New Mexico to the Hopi mesas in northeast Arizona. By AD 1300, we also knew, this village had been abandoned, never to be reoccupied. The very layout of the place, hidden from view, nestled with its back to the sheltering wall of the alcove, approached only via a steep bedrock slab, proclaimed a defensive urgency. Blissful though the ruin seemed to our modern eyes, its inhabitants had whiled away their last decades here in the grips of a perpetual fear.

The cliff behind the room block was covered with pictographs. Handprints in red and white, in three different styles: the "normal" kind, imprinted by an adult or youth who had smeared his palm with ocher (red) or kaolin (white), then pressed it against the wall; but also the "skeletal" variety, in which every bone in the hand seemed to be delineated as if by X-ray; as well as the "negative" print, crafted by a resident who had filled her mouth with masticated paint, flattened her palm against the wall, and spat a fine spray against the back of her hand, leaving a five-fingered outline to declare her witness.

There were also "lizard men" in red, cream, and orange. Chimerical creatures with human heads and trunks but reptilian appendages, they seemed to be caught in the act of scampering up the arching wall, as if fleeing some unfathomable predicament.

The casual visitor to such a ruin makes an easy mistake (as I often had myself, before I had learned more about rock art), which is to assume that the pictographs and the buildings were made by the same people. Now we could see that the walls of several rooms, where they came flush to the natural alcove, eclipsed the paintings behind them. The pictographs were older than the village; how much older, we could not say, but all three of us had visited ruins in other corners of the Southwest where we knew that the art predated the structures by at least several thousand years.

Over the years, Greg, Vaughn, and I had found literally hundreds of Anasazi ruins in the backcountry. Yet the thrill of coming upon a new one—especially one so beautiful as this—was undiminished. And this discovery, in the first two hours of our long trek on the Comb, had an added piquancy, in the reflection that, in all likelihood, very few non–Native Americans had ever stumbled across this village tucked inside the most obscure of dead-end canyons.

Thirty feet above the round tower, another alcove housed more structures. The only way up was via an Anasazi staircase—a hand-and-toe trail up the wall that had been carved by some architect wielding a hard pounding stone. Greg, the best climber in our trio, decided to have a look. The steps had weathered out over the centuries, and a few were simply missing, where patches of rock had flaked loose from the cliff. The trail was steep, approaching eighty degrees. Greg inched his way up as Vaughn and I watched him uneasily. He paused twenty feet up, momentarily stumped by a blank in the staircase. "Remember," Vaughn murmured, "you gotta reverse those moves."

With a deft scuttle, Greg gained the ledge. He spent twenty minutes exploring this lofty suburb of the prehistoric town, finding a granary in which the ancients had stored their corn—the most precious substance in the world, in the hard times around AD 1250. The whole upper ruin was fronted by a tall windowless wall facing west, into which loopholes had been inserted. Peering through these cylindrical tubes, which pointed in various directions, Greg saw how the Anasazi could have spied on intruders without being seen themselves. Here, in the upper level of the ruin, the paranoia of the long-vanished dwellers, driven to a marginal existence, still screamed from the very architecture.

Greg started down, as Vaughn and I stood below, our hands raised, offering a no doubt worthless "spot." The moves were indeed hard to reverse. "This is scary," Greg whispered, his left toe probing the precipice for the next shallow indentation. "Really scary." Vaughn and I kept our silence, sharing the same foreboding. A fall, a broken ankle, and the wonderful journey that we had planned for a year and a half might be over before it had really gotten started.

But Greg found the holds. As he reached terra firma, he let out a sigh of relief. "Nice job," I muttered. We hoisted our day packs and headed on.

The Comb Ridge is a true topographic anomaly. In geological terms, it is a monocline—a single fold in the earth's crust—created by a cataclysmic slippage of deep-buried tectonic plates some 65 million years ago. Coincidentally, the slippage occurred at the same time as the

Starting in the south near Kayenta, Arizona, Comb Ridge runs northward for over a hundred miles.

asteroid that plunged into the ocean off present-day Yucatán launched the mass extinction of the dinosaurs. (In the summer of 2004, just before we set out on our trek, the fossilized bones of a birdlike dinosaur, discovered only the year before, were excavated from the Comb under the aegis of the Bureau of Land Management.) That violent upheaval in the late Cretaceous has left a striking scar across the desert landscape of the Southwest: an upthrust ridge of sandstone—virtually a mini-mountain range—that stretches almost unbroken a hundred miles from just east of Kayenta, Arizona, to some ten miles west of Blanding, Utah. There is no other rock ridge like the Comb anywhere in the United States. From its southern end the crest sets out on an east–northeast vector and then gradually and gracefully bends to the north. Through its last sixty miles, the Comb swoops in a dead-straight line from south to north, before petering out in the twin creeks of Whiskers Draw.

Although the Comb varies in character along its swooping arc, certain aspects of it remain rigidly uniform. The east side of the ridge is relatively gentle, rising in slabs and terraces that range in angle from about twenty degrees to a maximum of fifty. The west flank, however, is a sheer precipice, plunging from the crest to the base at angles never much less than vertical. The scale of the Comb is not colossal: its ridgeline looms only 300 to 900 feet above the plains and shallow washes surrounding it on either side, with an average relief of 600 feet. But what the crest lacks in height, it makes up in ruggedness. No smooth arête, the ridge swoops to sharp summits and dips to V-notch cols with relentless regularity. To hike the Comb is to run a gauntlet of up-and-down severities, with the precipice lurking on one hand, the fiendishly convoluted bedrock slabs on the other—always at a sideways, ankle-wrenching pitch. There is not a single mile of established trail in the Comb's hundred-mile reach.

It is difficult to ascertain who named this bizarre wrinkle in the earth's crust. The earliest reference to it in print that I was able to come up with is an allusion to the Comb Wash—the tributary of the San Juan River that flows just west of the ridge—in a March 31, 1880, diary entry of Mormon pioneer Platte Lyman. In a retrospective account of the Mormon settling of southeast Utah, George Hobbs, Lyman's contemporary, wrote:

> *Our traveling east the next day brought us to Comb Wash. This wash derives its name from a particular cliff about thirty miles*

long on its east side which is scalloped out resembling a comb to some extent and here we came face to face with that cliff.

The only possible reason to question Hobbs's veracity is that his narrative was not published until 1919. Almost four decades of reflection could conceivably have corrupted the pioneer's memory.

I had also heard a persistent rumor that the Comb Ridge was actually named after an explorer named Macomb. In a 1938 work, *San Juan Country*, the geologist Herbert Gregory identifies the shallow, intermittent tributary of the San Juan River flowing just west of Bluff, Utah, now known as Cottonwood Wash, as having formerly been called "Macomb's Wash." Today's Comb Wash parallels Cottonwood, seven miles farther west.

Who was Macomb? In 1859, in response to Brigham Young's new Mormon empire in Utah, the U.S. Topographical Corps sent out Captain John H. Macomb to explore a vast, unknown tract northwest of Santa Fe. Making a long, ambitious loop, Macomb's party reached the junction of the Green and Colorado Rivers, in today's Canyonlands National Park. On their return, in late August and early September, the team passed east of the Abajo Mountains, and then followed a valley straight south to the San Juan River, which they ascended for more than a hundred miles on their way back to Santa Fe.

Between the Abajos and the San Juan, Macomb's team almost certainly saw, and may have named, Comb Ridge. The expedition report's map, however, indicates no such feature, nor does the text allude to it. Macomb himself was not impressed with this wild country. "I cannot conceive," he wrote, "of a more worthless and impracticable region than the one we now found ourselves in." The geologist in the party, John S. Newberry, who wrote most of the report, was of a different mind. Describing the view from near the junction of their southward-flowing tributary and the San Juan, Newberry extolled the "striking and impressive" features and "the walls and towers of some Cyclopean city hitherto undiscovered." A woodcut in the report, as we would later discover, looks very like the vista west from Comb Ridge where it is bisected by the San Juan, with the distant buttes of Monument Valley visible on the far left.

Yet Macomb records the longitude in which the team struck the San Juan as 109° 24' 43" W. This is almost eighteen minutes of longitude, or eleven miles, east of Comb Ridge, and accords most nearly not with Cottonwood Creek (as Gregory insisted), but with Recapture Creek east of Bluff. At the distance of nearly a century and a half, then, the question of who named Comb Ridge and what the appellation means may be insoluble.

As the 1859 party passed through this wilderness, Newberry was fascinated by the abundant vestiges of the ancients. Along the full hundred miles of the San Juan, he would later rave, "We were never out of sight of ruins." Macomb seems to have been less interested. Speculating briefly on the fate of the vanished Indians who had built these cliff dwellings and pueblos, he concluded that they must have starved or frozen to death.

The idea for our trip came one day in January 2003. Driving along U.S. Highway 160 between Dinnehotso and Kayenta on the Navajo Reservation, Vaughn Hadenfeldt and I gazed out the starboard window at the bluish billowing crests, one after another, that filed past our view, only three miles away across the dry arroyo of Laguna Creek. "Wonder if anybody's ever hiked the whole of the Comb," Vaughn mused.

I stared at the sandstone billows. "Wow. . . . Man, we should do it!" Turns out Vaughn had had the idea in the back of his mind for years. It had never before occurred to me—but in that instant, a traverse of the Comb Ridge seemed like the most appealing of possible projects in the Southwest, the landscape that both of us loved better than any other place on Earth.

The founder of Far Out Expeditions, based in Bluff, Vaughn was thoroughly familiar with the twenty-mile stretch of the Comb that lies between Utah State Highways 95 and 163, the only paved highways that bisect the monocline. He had guided many a client to such well-known Anasazi ruins as Monarch and Fishmouth Caves. The nearest prehistoric site on the Comb, in fact, lies only six miles from Vaughn's house.

I too had hiked many sections of this relatively accessible segment of the Comb, but always on day trips launched from pullouts on the dirt road that follows Butler Wash along the east side of the escarpment. Some of these were easy outings: at a brisk pace, for instance, you can hike from the car to Monarch Cave in only half an hour.

Nearly two-thirds of the Comb Ridge, however, lies on the Navajo

Reservation. To hike anywhere on the rez, you have to obtain a permit from the Navajo Nation headquarters in Window Rock, Arizona. Because of this minor bureaucratic hurdle, but also because for too many squeamish Anglos, the reservation has a slightly intimidating, Third-World feel about it, those southern sixty-five miles of the Comb remain all but unvisited by recreationists. Over the years, Vaughn and I had made a few forays into the region, but we could honestly say that we didn't know the Navajo stretch of the Comb very well at all.

Still gliding toward Kayenta in Vaughn's truck that January day, we gazed at the swooping crests on the right with a wild new longing. Two thumbs on the steering wheel, Vaughn said, "The big problem would be water."

"No kidding."

"We might have to cache some beforehand."

The first task, of course, was to find out if the complete traverse of the Comb Ridge had already been accomplished. During the next year, Vaughn and I queried every archaeologist, guide, and wilderness buff who might know. To our dawning joy, the universal verdict was negative. No one had heard even a rumor about the Comb being hiked in a single push. That fact itself seemed extraordinary. In an age when more or less arbitrarily defined marathon hikes such as the Appalachian and Continental Divide Trails attract hordes of enthusiasts (in the case of the former route, thousands every year), here was a naturally defined challenge that no one seemed to have responded to. As a climber, I knew that virtually every mountain range in the contiguous United States had long since been traversed from end to end—even such daunting massifs as the Tetons and the Palisades group in the Sierra Nevada.

From the start, Vaughn and I agreed that the third member of our expedition should be Greg Child. An Aussie who had emigrated to the United States in 1980, Greg is one of the outstanding mountaineers of his generation. He has climbed not only Everest and K2 (the latter by the seldom-essayed north ridge) but has spearheaded many big wall climbs in the remote ranges of Alaska, Pakistan, and Nepal. One of Greg's most impressive feats was the second ascent, in 1986, of Gasherbrum IV in the Karakoram; the first ascent twenty-eight years earlier by the legendary Italians Walter Bonatti and Carlo Mauri had been hailed as the finest climb yet accomplished at altitudes approaching 8000 meters (26,240 feet).

During the last five years, Greg—who lives upstream from Moab in Castle Valley, Utah—had fallen under the spell of the canyon country, largely (at first) nudged by invitations to join me on ruin- and rock-art-hunting rambles. Both Vaughn and I had been serious climbers in our twenties and thirties but in subsequent years had let our alpine skills grow rusty. On the other hand, Greg, in his mid-forties, was still climbing at a world-class level. From the start, Greg proved to have a keen natural eye for the stray arrowhead half-smothered in sand, for the faint markings on a far sandstone boulder that betokened a little-known rock art panel. And his technical expertise allowed Vaughn and me to gain access to certain ruins that we wouldn't have had the nerve to tackle on our own. Around many a campfire on Cedar Mesa, we had found that we had a congenial three-way rapport. We should, we thought, make up the ideal team for the Comb Ridge.

Like adventurers the world over, at first we kept our project secret, for fear someone else might steal the prize. The only reasonable seasons to hike in the Southwest are spring and fall. We planned our traverse first for the autumn of 2003 and then for the following spring, having to postpone the journey twice because we could not juggle our jobs and schedules. Meanwhile our secret leaked out, thanks to our not-so-subtle interrogations of the cognoscenti as to whether the Comb had ever been through-hiked. To our relief, when we finally set out on September 1, 2004, no one else had yet seen fit to try to beat us to the first traverse.

Despite thirteen expeditions to unclimbed routes and mountains in Alaska and the Yukon, I had never backpacked in a single jaunt for more than forty-five miles. The most extensive of those treks had proved a grim ordeal—a circuitous six-day escape from the Kichatna Spires in October 1966 through a winter-struck wilderness of glaciers, alder thickets, and tundra bogs, carrying seventy-five-pound packs, fording two rivers that had nearly drowned previous explorers, and coming to the near edge of hypothermia. In his late teens and early twenties, with an equally fanatic buddy, Vaughn had performed several hundred-mile backpacks in the Wind Rivers of Wyoming, the Beartooths of Montana, and the Sawtooths of Idaho, perfecting an intensely spartan style as they carried food for a month in hundred-pound packs, supplementing their starvation rations with trout caught in mountain streams. On expeditions in Asia, Greg had endured several hike-ins of upward of a hundred miles, sometimes through trackless rain forest, albeit reinforced by porters carrying their own towering loads.

In part because all three of us—even Greg—had gotten older and softer, we agreed to attack the Comb Ridge not in one grueling push with similarly outrageous loads but instead with the aid of resupply missions and pre-laid water caches. The main reason for this compromise in style, however, was that we did not want to bomb from one end of the Comb to the other as fast as we could but to take our time, seeking out the vestiges of Navajo and Anasazi presence that bear witness to the rich human history of this knife-edge of sandstone slashing across the Southwest. Ours was to be a cultural pilgrimage as much as an athletic one.

Five roads cut through the Comb Ridge in the course of its hundred-mile jaunt. Two are the aforementioned Utah State Highways 95 and 163. The other three are dirt tracks on the Navajo Reservation, two of them lying within the first four miles as the Comb makes a pair of geologic hiccups before launching out in earnest. We would arrange to be resupplied at four of these road intersections. If all went well, we would never have to carry more than five or six days' worth of food at a time.

Yet as Vaughn had pointed out that January day in 2003, water would be the big problem. Especially along the southern half of the Comb, springs and potholes looked to be in drastically short supply. Studying the maps like scholars of medieval manuscripts, we identified three spots where a cache of water deposited before the trip might spell the difference between continuing our journey or aborting it. In the spring of 2004, four months before we set out, I made several short day hikes into key corners of the Comb on the reservation to make sure that springs indicated on the maps had not dried up.

On day trips in the Southwest, I had never carried more than four quarts of water on even the most grueling outings. Now we reckoned that we would need a minimum of six quarts per man for each twenty-four-hour period. In the end, suffering under the ninety-degree temperatures that persisted through most of our hike, we sometimes drank nine or ten quarts per man per full day and night (including the water used to cook dinner and breakfast) and still felt our tongues parch with thirst. On several awful stretches, we carried three gallons of water apiece—twenty-four sloshing pounds of dead weight, in addition to all our gear and food.

In the days just before starting our hike, Vaughn and I hit the Durango, Colorado, Wal-Mart to buy spacious Rubbermaid containers and two-and-a-half-gallon jugs of so-called artesian water. Laying our three caches in the backcountry, however, was a more delicate business than simply driving out on rutted dirt roads and plunking our H_2O behind some camouflaging boulder. Our Window Rock permit ostensibly gave us the right to hike anywhere along the sixty-five miles of Comb Ridge that lie on the reservation. But Navajos are fiercely individualistic people. That permit could prove a worthless piece of paper in the hands of a sheepherder who considered our jaunt across his grazing land an act of blatant trespassing.

So on August 30 we hired a Navajo guide named Ramon Redhouse out of Kayenta to serve as our cache-laying liaison. The very start of the Comb rises out of a basin surrounded by cliffs on three sides, a mere four miles east of Kayenta. Peeking over a ridge on one of my spring recon hikes, I had seen that a tidy, well-kept "camp" or homestead centered that basin. As I watched through binoculars, a very old woman dressed in traditional garb emerged from her hogan—a classic specimen of the hexagonal traditional Navajo domicile—to toss a pail of dishwater onto the dirt. Now Ramon revealed to us that this family was the Begays (a name as common among the Navajo as Smith or Jones is in the Anglo phone book), and that, while they were kindly folks, they did not appreciate "tourists" wandering across their property. We would instead gain access to the southern butt-end of the Comb from a mile or so northeast of the Begay spread.

To break ourselves in as gently as possible, and to test (so to speak) the waters, or absence thereof, in this drought-stricken desert, we hoped to lay our first cache within the first few miles of our hike. In Vaughn's truck, with Ramon, we trundled up the driveway of the next Navajo camp northeast of the Begays', and then waited for some inhabitant to emerge. Even among Navajos, it can be rude to go up and knock on somebody else's door; for Anglos, it is an outright faux pas.

Within a few minutes, a fiftyish, leather-faced gent came out of his trailer home. Though Mr. Parrish spoke English, he and Ramon conversed alternately in that language and in Diné, the Navajo tongue. No, he wouldn't mind if we left some water just around the bend, where the first of the five road cuts sliced through the Comb. What

Mr. Parrish could understand if we wanted to hike over the Comb to go hunt a deer, but to walk it all the way to Blanding? He shook his head and wished us luck.

the three of us might be up to, however, baffled the man. In Diné, Mr. Parrish allowed as how he could see going up on the cliff to hunt deer. But just to walk . . . ? I handed the man fifty dollars, shook his limp hand, and thanked him for his help.

We hoped to deposit our second cache some thirteen miles farther along the Comb at the base of its northwestern precipice. The previous spring I had scouted a tricky but doable scramble from the crest 500 feet down to a scattering of rocks at the foot of the cliff. Now we set out on the faint track, marked on the USGS quads as "unimproved road," that paralleled the Comb as it traversed Cane Valley. Ramon had driven this road before in his own pickup, but he had also once gotten his vehicle stuck up to the doors in quicksand on this stretch.

With Vaughn at the wheel, we managed eight miles of track before we hit a patch where sand dunes had drifted across the road. We got out and walked the several hundred yards. "I don't like it," Vaughn said. "Be pretty easy to get hung up here." A truck stuck in the sand could mean a week's delay in our trip. We turned around and drove back almost all the way to Kayenta.

In the end we had to make a far-ranging loop of sixty miles, back to the highway and through Monument Valley, to cover the mere five that lurked between the sand dunes and the location of our second water cache. As we drove, Ramon regaled us with lore. In Diné, the name for the Comb, he said, was *Saba'naha*—prosaically enough, Gray or Tan Ridge. At one point, on another dirt road, we drove past an immature golden eagle perched on a nearby rock. It seemed odd that the bird wasn't spooked by our vehicle's noise and dust but instead sat there immobile.

I knew that traditional Navajos set great store by animal omens, but I wasn't sure how fully the worldly Ramon, accustomed to guiding tenderfeet through Monument Valley, embraced those beliefs. As we rounded a curve and reentered Cane Valley from the north, a coyote loped across the road ahead of us.

"Is that bad luck?" I asked, half-teasing.

"No, he was going south," answered Ramon, dead serious. "If he was going north, that'd be a pretty bad sign."

The niche I had identified for our cache the previous spring lay only half a mile away from another Navajo camp, comprising a scattering of dwellings, a fenced yard, and a livestock tank brimming with fresh water from a windmill well. Vaughn and I prepared ourselves for another tête-à-tête like the one with Mr. Parrish, but Ramon took one look and said, "Nobody there. The folks've probably moved into town." ("Town" meant Kayenta.)

"How do you know?" I asked.

Ramon pointed. "Tumbleweed around the house. No sign of livestock. No dogs."

Relieved at the convenient absence of the local landlords, we stashed fifteen gallons of water behind a large boulder, taping shut the Rubbermaids and appending a note explaining our dependence on this stash during the coming weeks. Still, it was hard to shake a guilty sense that we were invading someone's backyard. We placed the cache with a certain furtive haste, as if fearing that someone (besides Ramon) was looking over our shoulders.

To deposit our third and last water cache, we crossed over the Comb on the northernmost of the three dirt-road traversals on the rez, and then pushed Vaughn's truck through the sagebrush along a series of vestigial tracks as we climbed the lower slopes of the Comb from the east. The cache spot was in the shade of the biggest juniper tree around (no boulders hereabouts), but as we tried to memorize the surroundings, we sensed that, ten days or so hence, approaching from above, it would be hard to tell this tree from any of fifty others scattered across the Comb's eastern apron.

About a quarter mile away from the juniper stood another lonely Navajo camp. Before dropping our water, we paid a visit to Chester and Rena Benally, who, though they lived in a frame house rather than a hogan, were traditional old-timers (we guessed they were in their seventies) who didn't speak a word of English.

The Benallys sat side by side on an old couch, while we occupied facing chairs. Throughout our half-hour chat, Chester held his left leg rigidly extended in the air, while he kneaded his calf muscles. I thought he was trying to relieve an old injury, but Ramon later told me that Chester's left leg was a wooden prosthesis. "Diabetes," he said matter-of-factly. "We get a lot of that on the reservation."

At the appropriate moment, I handed Rena fifty dollars. Without a word, she seized the bills, scuttled over to the bed, and tucked them under the pillow.

The whole conversation, of course, took place in Diné. Stony faced

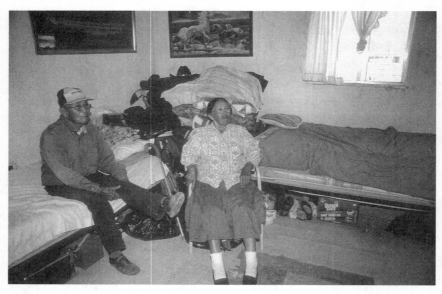

"If we see ravens circling, we'll know it's you people." Mr. and Mrs. Benally thought we'd get a bit too thirsty along the arid Comb.

and shy when we had entered the house, the Benallys were soon chuckling along with Ramon. It was only later that we learned what the banter was about. One of the first things Navajo strangers discuss is their clans. As Ramon later glossed the discourse, "Both Chester and I are Folded Arm clan. So he's my dad. She's Bitter Water born for Towering House, so she's my granddaughter, even though she must be forty years older than I am. That's what we were laughing about.

"A lot of teasin' goes on. That's how you break the ice."

Like Mr. Parrish, the Benallys thought our plan of hiking the Comb was crazy. "When I see the ravens circling, I'll know it's you guys," Chester had joshed.

As we drove away, I felt stunned by the isolation of the Benally ménage. Ramon regarded it as nothing extraordinary. "They truck their drinking water in from Goulding's," he said, alluding to the old trading post turned fashionable motel thirty-five miles away on the western edge of Monument Valley. "The water in the tank's only good for livestock.

"They never went to school. And, yeah—they've lived there all their lives."

That first day on the Comb, September 1, we poked along at a leisurely pace, dropping our packs once more to make an exploratory loop down to the base of the escarpment on the south, mainly in search of water holes. We were carrying only four quarts of the precious stuff per man, because the first of our caches, around the bend from Mr. Parrish's camp, was within easy reach. It had not rained anywhere in the Four Corners region during the previous ten days. We passed a dozen potholes that would have brimmed with water after a good downpour, but now every one was dry. Finally, almost at the base of the ridge, we found a narrow pocket in the bedrock that held a few gallons of tea-colored water. It was a heartening sight: that *any* hole in this desiccated wasteland could have resisted the ravages of solar evaporation boded well for our journey.

By mid-morning, the temperature had risen to ninety degrees Fahrenheit. "It's *hot*," said Greg, belaboring the obvious.

"Yepper," Vaughn replied. "We'll be burning the roofs of our mouths." This last a desert-rat hyperbole, the idea being that as you walk along panting, the sun reflecting off the slickrock can inflict ultraviolet damage even inside your mouth.

None of us had been able to do much hiking in the several weeks before the trip. We were counting on the Comb to whip us into shape. But I was dismayed to realize, after only four hours of hiking, that not only were my thighs starting to cramp, but I was getting hot spots on the balls of my feet. I hadn't had a blister in years of Southwest rambling, but now I begged a halt so I could tape up my feet.

Vaughn found us a campsite by mid-afternoon, in a hollow half-way up the Comb. The site's chief virtue was an east-facing cliff, in whose shade we could sprawl as the sun went down. Just before sunset, we climbed to a knob on the very crest and watched the landscape transmute to a blazing orange. From here we could see the smooth parabola of the Comb as it bent on and on into the northeast and sense just how long a voyage we had ahead of us. Sunset, in fact, would become our favorite time of day during the trip.

Mr. Parrish's camp lay directly below us. The reservation stretched to the dusky horizon on all sides. "*Lonely* country," I wrote in my diary. "The odd pickup rolling down dirt roads far away, sending up clouds of dust." At 7:45 PM the sun finally slipped behind Skeleton Mesa, some fifteen miles to the west. Over there, in the many-branching Tsegi Canyon system, an Anasazi paradise that includes two of the finest cliff dwellings in the Southwest, Betatakin and Keet Seel, I had enjoyed some seven or eight outings, including a pair of five-day backpacks, on each of which I never saw another Anglo.

We returned to camp and voraciously downed the tomato soup and macaroni and cheese that Vaughn cooked up for us. The moon, two days past full, rose suddenly at 9:30 PM over the Lukachukai Mountains to the southeast, another seldom-visited canyon labyrinth where I had spent eight days on a horse-packing trip in 1996, finding many Anasazi sites that few Anglos had ever beheld. Lurid orange, its craters and maria vivid in the clear sky, the moon performed its usual optical illusion of looking twice as big as it does when it wheels higher overhead.

It was so warm that we didn't bother pitching our one-man tents, instead simply stretching out on the bedrock in our super-light sleeping bags. It was the last night we would bivouac thus, for throughout the wee hours, tiny gnats and stingless mosquitoes whined about our heads, making sleep fitful at best. Even Vaughn, with his decades of camping in the Four Corners, had never suffered bugs like this in a dry September. We would spend days spinning improbable theories to explain their presence, which persisted throughout the long march.

A plume of windborne dust, hail, and rain slammed the Comb with a mud storm.

Our plan had been to follow the crest of the Comb as closely as we could, but by the second day, we could see that a literal ridgeline traverse was impossible. Many of the bulging lumps and fins—the teeth of the Comb—rose in seamless walls at angles of seventy or eighty degrees. On the northwest side the ridge often overhung the ledges below. We carried a thin climbing rope, but no hardware, so any technical gymnastics we might perform would amount to free soloing.

Instead, each day we improvised a circling, looping meander among the crests and crevices that convoluted this geological marvel. Most of the potholes and tanks (the cowboy term for a big natural pothole) that we would eventually find were located low on the southeastern and eastern slopes, so that for campsites we were sometimes forced almost to the foot of the Comb. We were drawn low, also, by the fact that the preponderance of Anasazi ruins and rock art was located on those lower shelves (no doubt in part because of the available water).

On our second day, however, we saw far more Navajo rock art than Anasazi. Some of it was little more than graffiti: dates as recent as 1982 (at 8:00 AM, in fact, though the day and month were unspecified), a pecked salutation that read "HELLO BESTY.CT," another guest-register entry in two lines:

Jim Birdsong, Farmington, NM, 1969
I was here too—Frosty Heath.

(Birdsong was plainly a Navajo name, but I wondered about old Frosty.)

Elsewhere in the Southwest, all three of us had found inscriptions that consisted of little more than strings of capital letters. We knew from historical accounts that some of these doodlings were the work of youths—Navajo here, Ute farther north—who, shortly after the turn of the twentieth century, having been taught the white man's alphabet in school, were practicing on the rocks. Thus at one gap in the ridge I stumbled upon the following string:

I
ABCDEFGHJK.

Alas, sandstone does not make a forgiving blackboard: the diligent kid who had left the "I" out of his ABCs had to stick it back in as a superscript.

Nearby, however, a string of characters looked like some hallucinatory mix of Roman, Sumerian, and Greek:

I would have given much to know what this teenage scribe had in mind, as I would the fellow who had scratched the name MALLORY in well-wrought capitals, but all backward and half upside-down, thus:

There were Navajo portraits of tough-looking dudes in cowboy hats, as well as full-sized honchos in profile, some of them X-rated. Mixed in with the Navajo stuff, far older and more darkly patinated, were animals and humanoids of Anasazi manufacture, carved not with metal tools but with chert flakes or quartzite pecking stones.

And here we saw what at first glance appeared to be several instances of shocking vandalism. A number of Anasazi petroglyphs (figures carved in the rock, as opposed to the painted pictographs) had been almost completely obliterated by the gouging of some sharp-edged tool, probably a chisel or an ax. A patent savagery seemed to emanate from the very violence of the gouging. Yet right next to a pair of wiped-out petroglyphs, the Navajo rock-art censors had left intact a bulbous Anasazi deer. Instead of effacing this figure, some chisel-wielding emender had made precise swipes that cut into the beast's head, neck, heart, genitals, and leg joints.

The first time I had seen a rock art panel defaced in this fashion had come on a San Juan River float trip in 1996, when our group had pulled to shore to hike to a rather famous site called the Desecrated Panel. There, thanks to a fortuitous overlapping of traditional Navajos with rafting guides in the 1950s, the true meaning of the apparently wanton vandalism had been passed down to Anglo comprehension.

On our second day on the Comb, then, as we stared at the viciously gouged petroglyphs, I had strong inklings (as did Vaughn) as

Navajo cowboy rock art. The numbers are probably personal ID cards.

to just what had gone on here, perhaps fifty years ago, perhaps longer, perhaps in the last decade or two. To explain the desecration, however, a little anthropology is in order.

❈

The Navajo insist that they have always lived in the Southwest—within the quadrangle, in fact, formed by the four sacred mountains: Sierra Blanca in southern Colorado, Mount Taylor in western New Mexico, the San Francisco Peaks near Flagstaff, Arizona, and Hesperus Peak in southwestern Colorado. But science begs to differ. Linguistically and culturally, the Navajo are classed as an Athapaskan people—along with their distant cousins the Apache, the two are the only Athapaskans in the Southwest. They are thus related to such other Athapaskans as the Chipewyan Indians of subarctic Canada, who roam the tundra and forest west of Hudson Bay. The languages of the Chipewyan and Navajo, in fact, remain so close that many words are mutually intelligible. And Helge Ingstad, the great Norwegian explorer who lived with the Chipewyans as a trapper for four years in the 1920s, recorded their legends of a long-ago exodus of a substantial portion of their people, who set off toward the south and never returned.

Nomads leave scant evidence of their passage on the ground; but no unambiguously Navajo campsite or artifact dating before 1500 has yet been found in the Southwest. Most anthropologists believe that the Navajo arrived in their present heartland no earlier than that date, though a few experts would push the advent back as far as 1400. We also know with certainty that the Anasazi, who had occupied the Southwest for at least several millennia, completely abandoned a huge sector of the Colorado Plateau around the Four Corners region just before 1300, emigrating en masse to the south and east.

Thus the conclusion is all but inescapable: when the Navajo arrived in the northern Southwest, the Anasazi were already gone. They had, of course, left behind abundant evidence of their dazzling civilization, especially in the form of well-preserved ruins and rock art. Even today, the Navajo have strong taboos about places of the dead: if an elder dies in his or her hogan, the home will often be abandoned or even burned to the ground. Those taboos kept the Navajo from entering—much less vandalizing—the Anasazi ruins they came across, leaving them in pristine condition when the first Spanish and Anglo-American explorers penetrated the Southwest.

What, then, could possibly explain the violent gouging of the Anasazi rock art that Vaughn, Greg, and I discovered on our second day on the Comb? Visiting Desecrated Panel on the San Juan during that float trip in 1996, I had seen the same sort of selective destruction: some petroglyphs completely effaced, some left intact, and others (in this case, humanoids) with heart, head, joints, and genitals precisely gouged. The fortuitous overlap had come in the late 1950s, when the founder of the rafting company with which I was floating the river had befriended the Navajos who lived on its left bank. Kenny Ross had been told that a large extended family had been stricken with some terrible disease. Calling in a shaman to attempt a cure, they had been told that the "rock writings from the sun people" were causing their illness. Attacking the rock art panel on the banks of the San Juan, only a few hundred yards from their hogans, had been an act of desperation, as the Navajo tried to save their own people from a wasting death.

It would not be our privilege to learn when or why or by whom the panels we found on the Comb had been similarly desecrated, but we could be pretty sure that the vandalizing had sprung from a kindred motive.

In general, the Navajo regard the Anasazi as having possessed extraordinary and even magical powers. The deepest exploration of this cultural cross-bedding by an Anglo scholar is in the pages of Robert S. McPherson's 1992 book, *Sacred Land, Sacred View: Navajo Perceptions of the Four Corners Region*. As research for his treatise, McPherson interviewed many old-timers on the Navajo Reservation, a good portion of whom are no longer alive. The results are fascinating.

Any hiker who has ever probed the slickrock canyons of the Four Corners region has been dumbstruck by the evidence, in the form of inaccessible cliff dwellings, that the Anasazi must have been master rock climbers. Climbers ourselves, Greg, Vaughn, and I had discovered many a prehistoric site high in some diminutive alcove that we could see no way to get to except by rappelling from the cliff top—a technique we can safely assume was not in the Anasazi arsenal. Arriving whenever they did in the Southwest, the Navajo too were stunned by the aerial feats of their predecessors. Thus arose the legends not only that the Anasazi were gifted climbers, but that they could fly. McPherson learned from one elder that the ancients had special "sticky feet" to aid their climbing; another told him that the

Anasazi "used shiny stones to slide up and down the rock walls." Yet others insisted that lizards and horned toads—noted for their ability to scuttle up vertical walls—were the descendants of the Anasazi.

In 1868 the U.S. government established the Navajo Reservation as a vast, zigzag-bordered tract covering much of northeastern Arizona and spilling into New Mexico (and later, into Utah). This reserve unfortunately surrounded (and thus, by federal fiat, incorporated) the three mesas on which the Hopi had been living for at least a thousand years. A separate, much smaller Hopi Reservation, smack in the middle of the Navajo Reservation, was not formally established until 1882. All this well-meaning but misguided legislation has created an intercultural conundrum whose legacy is nearly a century and a half of conflict and anguish. Successive acts of Congress have shifted the borders of both reservations over the years, in the process often dispossessing Natives (both Navajo and Hopi) from homesteads they had occupied for generations. Even today, despite much intermarriage, the Hopi and the Navajo maintain an edgy coexistence, and violence between the peoples occasionally breaks out.

Anthropologists are certain, moreover, that the Hopi, as well as the people living in the nineteen New Mexico pueblos ranging from Zuni to Taos, are the direct descendants of the Anasazi. The Hopi visit ruins and maintain shrines today in the Four Corners region, which their ancestors had abandoned by 1300, and many old stories detail that long-ago migration. Yet—as McPherson may have been the first scholar to discover—the Navajo adamantly deny that the Hopi are at all related to the Anasazi. In the Navajo view, they are two distinct peoples—no matter what the Hopi say about their forebears.

What might this belief serve? The answer is clear. The Navajo are convinced that the Anasazi abused their magical powers, angering their own gods, and were destroyed in retribution. Just as intriguingly, a majority of the elders whom McPherson interviewed believed that Anglo America was headed along the same arrogant path toward its own destruction. As one informant, Fred Yazzie, told McPherson in 1987:

> *Just like now, the Anglos are designing many things. They are making big guns and poison gas. Whatever will harm humans, they are designing. What happened then [with the Anasazi] I am relating to what is happening now. . . . Now the Anglos are going up to the moon and space. Whatever*

obstacle is in their way, they will not allow it to stop them.
Some are killed doing this and others return from their quest.
Do these people believe in the Holy Beings or God?

According to Yazzie, "The Anasazi built with ease houses in the cliffs. Their mind probably did all this and this was like a big competition between them. They started to fly and then got jealous of each other."

Said another informant, "They learned to fly . . . that is why their houses are in the cliffs . . . [but] the Holy Beings had their feelings hurt by it . . . [and] said it was not good and killed them off."

In the view of some elders Anasazi rock art itself embodies the ancients' abuse of their power. Of the petroglyph and pictograph panels in Canyon de Chelly, Mae Thompson told a scholar in 1986 that the depictions of "abstract" things such as wind and air, as well as "caricatures of animals," were particularly offensive. "The gods became angry, sent a whirlwind and fire, and destroyed life in the canyons and mesas. The black streaks of desert varnish that cover cliffs and rocks in the area are from the smoke and fire of this destruction." Beliefs such as Thompson's offer an alternative explanation to the one received by Kenny Ross on the San Juan as to the possible reason for the kind of desecration the three of us found on Comb Ridge.

The term Anasazi, first applied by the great archaeologist Alfred V. Kidder in 1936 and in standard use ever since, is a Navajo word meaning roughly "ancestral enemies." McPherson glosses *'anaa'* (the apostrophes representing glottal stops) as "war, alien, enemy" and *sází* as "ancestor, ancestral." In recent years, some Puebloans, particularly Hopi, have objected to the term. The Hopi would substitute their own name for the Old Ones, *Hisatsinom*, but the trouble is that other Puebloans have their own quite different names for their ancestors. Driven by liberal guilt, many younger archaeologists have started substituting the awkward catch-all designation "Ancestral Puebloans" for Anasazi. One might, however, object to "puebloan" as a Spanish word meaning simply "inhabitant of a town."

Recently, the National Park Service took this politically correct revisionism to an absurd (and in scholarly terms, harmful) extreme by refusing to stock in its gift shops any book with the term Anasazi in its title, regardless of when it was written. There was even talk of banning all books that used the term in their texts. This last straw finally provoked a counter-salvo, led mainly by senior Southwestern scholars, that erupted in a cry of outrage at the 2004 Pecos Conference in Bluff, Utah.

Some writers (myself included) have gone right on using Anasazi, despite the inevitable slaps on the wrists from self-righteous letters to editors. My view is that most people in history (and prehistory) have been named by their enemies, and we might as well accept the fact. "Eskimo" is an Algonquian Indian name, in happy usage until the 1980s, when we were all taught to say "Inuit" instead. For that matter, no designation could be more erroneous or illogical than Columbus's "Indian"—and yet Native Americans all over the country seem to feel little discomfort in referring to themselves and each other as Indians. Navajo, it should be pointed out, is a Tewa (Puebloan) word, meaning something like "those who make fields in the washes" (a very curious designation, since when the sedentary Puebloans first encountered the Navajo they were nomads, not farmers); but as of yet there is no brushfire movement underway to insist on Diné ("the People") instead of Navajo.

All this fuss over politically correct usage obscures a provocative hint embedded in the term Anasazi. If the Navajo regarded the Old Ones who could fly and build houses in the cliffs as "ancestral enemies," does that mean that the two people overlapped in the Southwest after all? The fact that we have not yet found a Navajo tent ring or arrowhead in the region dating from before 1500 does not prove these Athapaskans couldn't have reached the Southwest as much as two centuries earlier. As I was to learn from the very books I read as we trudged along the Comb, many old Navajo stories are still told about interacting with the Anasazi, even about watching their "enemies" abandon the Colorado Plateau.

At precisely 3:00 PM on our second day, we received our first resupply. This seemed absurdly early for such a refurbishing of food and gear—we had been backpacking, after all, for only a day and a half—but the accident of where the three dirt roads crossed the Comb dictated our logistics. We had enlisted an old friend from Bluff, Jim Hook, to perform these vital missions. Jim is the proprietor of Recapture Lodge, a comfy motel that for more than a decade had been one of my favorite places to stay in the Southwest. He had also, in 1988, become the first llama outfitter in the Four Corners area. On many trips Jim served as guide and llama wrangler for his clients; on others, he simply leased out to his clients animals that he had trained so well that, after a half-hour lesson, even a rookie could handle them in the backcountry. In this latter fashion, five times over the last fifteen years, I had rented Jim's llamas and set out on halcyon trips lasting from five to eight days.

During his first years in Bluff, Jim and his wife, Luanne, had hiked all over the glorious country west and south of Bluff; but by 2004, the couple had produced four rambunctious young 'uns (three girls and a boy), forcing a somewhat more sedentary lifestyle onto the former vagabonds. Now, on September 2, Jim drove up in his SUV, with our goodies in the back, and five-year-old Thomas as his copilot.

Our resupply system was the soul of luxury. During the last few days before the trip, guided by Vaughn's tried-and-true schemes, in a frenzy of measuring and bagging, we had stashed each customized segment of Comb rations into its own carefully labeled Rubbermaid. Every meal was prepackaged and ready to seize as the occasion demanded. And while the gear we were carrying in our already bulging backpacks was as lightweight as we could make it, we had given Jim duffels filled with substitute gear we might swap off at each resupply, from heavier sleeping bags to backup Therm-a-Rest pads to unexposed film to a small library of books.

Young Thomas was a bit bewildered by our system. As Jim glided to a halt beside the three backpackers, sprawled in the only handy patch of cliff shade, the five-year-old took one look at the soaring continuation of the Comb that rose over our right shoulders, another at the mountain of stuff in the backseat, and said to his dad, "How are they going to get it all up there?"

We reorganized for an hour. The next stretch of Comb called for five days of food, which might prove to be our longest unaided segment. And by now we were seriously worried about the water problem. Our second cache of bottled aqua lay eleven miles ahead as the crow flies; it could well take us three days to cover that stretch. Now, therefore, we loaded our backpacks not only with five days of grub, but with twelve quarts of water per man—the minimum, in the kind of heat we were enduring, for two days of lumbering progress. Five days' worth of food and stove fuel weighed about fourteen pounds per man, and the twelve quarts of water meant twenty-four pounds apiece. Grateful though we were for Jim's resupply, it meant that we had just added nearly forty pounds apiece to our burdens.

We groaned and cursed as we wrenched these "pigs" (as climbers designate heavy packs) to a perch on a bended knee, and then pivoted into the straitjacket of shoulder straps and waist belt. We waved good-bye to the SUV. Jim said later that as Thomas had watched us stagger toward the foot of the steep crest of sandstone where the Comb recommenced in earnest, he said, "They look like good buddies."

We managed only a mile during the remainder of the afternoon. I guessed I was carrying seventy-five to eighty pounds, more than I had backpacked in at least a decade, maybe two. Vaughn's pack was even heavier. As we angled up a ramp toward a low col between a pair of Comb teeth where we hoped to camp, I felt an intolerable strain on my thighs, calves, and shoulders. It seemed impossible with loads like these to do any real scrambling: even this gentle ramp walk seemed an agony. For the first time, dark doubts assailed my thoughts: *I'm not at all sure if we can pull off this traverse.*

At last we tossed the pigs down at the saddle between crests labeled 5805' and 5945' on the map. In two days we had covered about eleven miles of hiking but gained only four as the crow flies. Four out of a hundred: a mere one twenty-fifth of the gauntlet we had proposed for ourselves. I felt a numb discouragement.

The col would have been a nice place to camp under normal circumstances, but now a stiff wind sprang up out of the south. It cooled us off but rendered our flimsy one-man tents unpitchable on the bedrock. Any loose object carelessly laid down—a cap, a tent fly, even a food bag—was in danger of being seized by the gusts and flung over the precipice to the northwest. We retreated a hundred yards below the col and set up camp in a sandy hollow. I spent the hour before sunset poking around the little basin enclosed by the twin crests. Vaughn had pointed out the ruins of an old Navajo hogan—the female kind, a round circle of stones with the door facing east, as opposed to the male variety, the more prevalent wooden forked-stick hogan. I strolled through and around this forlorn site, wondering how old it was.

Wind or no wind, we climbed back to the col to watch the sunset. It was nearing the horizon just left of the weird volcanic plug called Agathla, a gray pinnacle rising more than a thousand feet from its base, about eight miles west of us. Out there on the overgrazed prairie, the wind was whipping up dust storms, and as the sun inched lower, it turned orange and then ruddy red. Then, at the last minute, an amazing sight materialized. The only cloud in the sky, a cirrus anomaly directly above the sun, was suddenly lit up, but only along the edges, in a continuous flat disk of fiery yellow. It looked like a flying saucer limned by its own eerie glow, or like some cosmic smoke ring wafted aloft by one of the Holy Beings. None of us had ever seen the like. And it lasted only for four or five minutes. Greg fired off a roll of film, trying to catch the evanescent glory of that day-closing apparition in the sky.

As we started out the next morning, our only consolation was that our packs were perhaps eight to ten pounds lighter, thanks to the water we had drunk and the dinner and breakfast consumed. Jim Hook had told us that the forecast was for a drop in temperature of about ten degrees, but if the world around us had cooled off, we had yet to detect the change. The wind, which had blown all night, intensified in the morning, although now it shifted direction, hurtling out of the southwest—directly behind our backs, thank God. By mid-morning, it streamed at a steady thirty miles an hour, with gusts over forty. With all the sand carried by the wind, the crystalline landscape through which we had set out three days earlier had bleared to a gray-brown smudge. Buttes and rock formations only a few miles away were barely visible in the maelstrom. As we hiked, hunched forward to counterbalance our monster loads, we tasted sand in our teeth. As Vaughn pointed out, the wind itself dehydrated us, wicking away our sweat as fast as we could exude it from our pores.

A taciturn fellow at all times, Vaughn was given to lapsing into a rural drawl, the likes of which I had never heard before I met him. After several years of being tickled to hear such soliloquies, I asked him where the idiom came from. Turns out Vaughn had spent some of his high school summers working as a hand on ranches near Fort Collins, Colorado, that were run by second-generation Swedes. It was their twang that, decades later, was still firmly lodged in his head. Just the previous afternoon, for instance, as we strode across a sand dune, Vaughn had spontaneously lamented, "We haven't even found any arryheads."

As we hiked, all three of us constantly scanned the ground ahead of us, alert for glimpses of ancient artifacts. Vaughn, however, was a master at this craft: he had, in fact, the finest eye for detail on the ground of any friend I had ever hiked with. So far we had already spotted hundreds of potsherds, but it was lithics (as archaeologists categorize the debris left by makers of chert and obsidian tools) that Vaughn lived for.

An atlatl dart point or arrowhead of the milky stone commonly seen along the Comb

Thus, on September 3, when, only fifteen minutes into our trudge, Greg burst out, "There's one!" Vaughn could not resist exclaiming, "I saw it, too!" Greg stooped to pick up a beautiful projectile point, a sharpened piece of milky white chalcedony with jets of red streaking through the stone. Its stem was broken off, but Vaughn knew from its size and shape that the tool was in fact a dart point, not an "arryhead."

In the Southwest, the Anasazi did not invent (or get introduced to) the bow and arrow until sometime after AD 500. Before that, for millennia, hunters and warriors had used the atlatl, or spear-thrower—an ingenious device independently discovered by natives all over the world. The Anasazi version consisted of a wooden stick grooved at one end with a shallow trough. A pair of finger loops, usually made of yucca or rawhide, allowed the wielder to hold the thrower in one hand. The dart itself was a longer, lighter stick hafted to a stone point, and then laid in the grooved trough of the throwing stick. The hunter held the implement over his head, took a step or two or even a little run, and flung the throwing stick violently forward, more or less in the motion of a javelin tosser—except that he kept hold of the throwing stick, releasing only the dart. The extra torque created by, in effect, lengthening one's throwing arm imparted a huge mechanical advantage to the winging dart. Experiments with modern facsimiles reveal that an atlatl dart could easily cover a hundred yards or more and strike with such force that it might pass completely through the body of a deer or bighorn sheep.

You can't directly date a piece of stone found in the sand, like the one Greg had spied; but the style and size of the projectile point are diagnostic of whether it is an atlatl dart or a true arrowhead. In general, dart points are longer and bigger than arrowheads, and arrowheads themselves shrink in size through the centuries up to the AD 1300 abandonment, probably because the Anasazi slowly hunted the big game to near-extinction. The lithic point Greg fondled in his fingers was, we thus knew, a minimum of 1500 years old.

I've never met a Southwestern aficionado, even a professional archaeologist, who, when pressed on the subject, would not admit that he had kept the first several arrowheads or dart points he ever found. By now, however, Greg, Vaughn, and I had long cured ourselves of the collector's nasty habit. We fondled and photographed the prettiest things we discovered on the ground, but left every single potsherd and chert flake where we found it. Vaughn sometimes even buried a point in the sand, to make it less likely that the next passerby would pick it up and stick it in his pocket. Quite aside from the ethics of our "outdoor museum" (as Vaughn and several cronies had named the artifact-handling regimen they had concocted some two decades before), we knew that it was illegal—a violation of the 1906 Antiquities Act—to keep even the most insignificant ancient artifact found on federal land, or for that matter, on the Navajo Reservation.

During our many days together in the canyon country, the three of us had freely admitted that lithic-spotting (as well as potsherd- and rock art–finding) was a competitive sport. Vaughn's "I saw it, too!" was a telltale outburst of a man who prided himself on noticing stuff the rest of us walked heedlessly past. Thus, later that wind-bleared day, when I stumbled upon a perfect gray-green arrowhead, the finest point we would find on the whole trip, I barely managed to conceal my glee while Vaughn circled the area, fuming in a private funk as he sought some other lithic that might trump my chance find.

We made other discoveries that day, including several panels of curious Anasazi rock art: lizard men; a bighorn sheep with its feet on backward; a petroglyphic web or maze (interpreted by the Hopi sometimes as a migration map of the ancestors); an animal outlined in red paint, anomalously facing the viewer (nearly all Anasazi "zoomorphs"—depictions of animals real or mythic—are seen in profile) and looking for all the world like a koala bear. But we also exhausted ourselves winding in and out of the lumps and teeth near the crest of the Comb. At one point, we tried to "sneak" an unclimbable bump on the northwest side, but the ledge petered out in blank precipice. We had to backtrack, scramble across several tricky fins, and ultimately descend almost to the base of the Comb on the southeast just to gain half a mile.

Our loads were killing us, and the wind showed no sign of letting up. As the universe grayed further and closed tighter around us, we recognized that we were hiking through a veritable sandstorm. No matter how much we drank, our urine flowed a darkish yellow, the sure sign of dehydration. And all day, we found not a single pothole cradling even the skankiest few gallons of fetid water.

We were constantly thirsty. The day before, we had instituted our "beer fine." Because the whole of the Navajo Reservation is dry, we allowed ourselves not a single drop of alcohol among our provisions. This was a sore privation, for, car camping on Cedar Mesa, the three of us loved nothing better, after a long day in the canyons, than to flop down in the shade of a juniper and pop a brewski kept chilled in the backseat cooler. I favored cans of Tecate, while Vaughn swore by Moosehead.

Now, we agreed, each time one of us uttered the word "beer," he was fined a dollar. We had enough self-control not to blurt out the taboo word on purpose, but then one of us would slip. "Boy, did we all get wasted at Kitty and Jay's wedding," Greg would reminisce. "We must've gone through six cases of beer between—"

"Cases of what?" Vaughn would interrupt.

"Ah, shit!"

"That's four dollars just today."

By the end of our journey, we had lost track of the precise magnitude of the accumulated fines, but Greg and I acknowledged that we were far deeper in debt than the better-disciplined Vaughn.

On September 3, we called it a day at 4:30 PM. In eight and a half hours, we had wound some nine miles, gaining a creditable seven as the crow flies. Our campsite was low on the southeast slope, behind a four-foot-high cliff facing east that blocked much of the wind. "Man, I'm whupped!" Vaughn swore as he threw down his pig. In the partial shelter of our wall, we managed to cook up a dispirited dinner of French onion soup and freeze-dried goulash. As I sat in the lee of the wall, spooning soup from my bowl, I tasted sand. There was sand in my ears, sand in my eyes, a tangled mélange of sand and sweaty hair atop my head.

We got inside our tents early. The wind shook them so fiercely, it was hard to get to sleep, no matter how tired we were. At last I drifted off. And when I woke, sometime in the wee hours, in the pitch dark before moonrise, I heard the most joyous of possible sounds. Not the flapping of the tent, to which I had finally grown accustomed. No—a steady pitter-patter—the sound of rain splattering on the tent fly. Rain, our deliverance!

ROUNDING MONUMENT VALLEY

IN THE DESERT, A TYPICAL RAINSTORM arrives in a sudden afternoon burst, and then clears out before sunset. This all-night drizzle was something different. We were up at 6:45 AM on September 4. As if to tempt fate, I had pitched my tent right in the bedrock channel of a little wash. I had barely gotten my sleeping bag and tent packed up, while Vaughn cooked breakfast in the lee of our four-foot cliff, when an ominous mass of dark clouds came blasting in from the west. All at once lightning bolts were tearing through the sky, some striking within a mile of our camp. Lightning, at dawn! There was nothing to do but hunker beside the cliff and wait it out. And now the floodgates unleashed: the gentle patter of the night (a female rain, as the Navajo call it) transmuted into an angry, lashing downpour (masculine in spades, according to the Navajo).

The lightning strikes were a bit unnerving, but at least we had not camped right on the vulnerable crest of the Comb. Had we found ourselves in some mountain range, attempting to climb a peak, a storm such as this would have dictated retreat. Instead, across the parched reservation, it was a godsend. The rain kept coming and coming: every rill in the slope started to run with its own miniature flash flood. Greg said, "We don't need to carry all this goddamned water," then, without a second thought, opened a couple of bottles and poured their contents out onto the ground.

"Wait—" I blurted. The act of dumping water—water you had lugged painfully on your back for more than eight hours the day before—seemed obscene. But Greg was right. For the next several days, at least, and maybe longer, all our water problems were solved.

We set out at 8:30 in a joyous frame of mind. The temperature had dropped some forty degrees since the day before. Greg, who had left all his warmer clothes in Jim Hook's resupply van, was wearing every item he carried. I myself had a Gore-Tex jacket, rain pants, and fleece cap on, with the jacket hood closed tight around my eyes and nose.

Vaughn was energized by the deluge, setting out at a pace that was almost a jog. When I pleaded with him to slow down, he turned and proclaimed, "I feel good!" Then, glancing up at the turbulent sky, he bellowed, "Whoo, doggies!"—not Swedish rancher talk, but stockdrive cowboy.

It rained hard for two hours straight. At the end of the downpour, I guessed that a total of half an inch had fallen. If so, that represented something like one-fifteenth of the region's annual precipitation. As always in the desert, the rain unlocked the vegetation's dormant odors, particularly the pungent tang of the sagebrush. We hiked on, Greg and I trying to keep up with Vaughn, at the fastest pace we had yet marshaled. Perhaps, I mused, we were starting to get in shape.

There was still lightning crashing down on the plains to the south and east, but in the west a rim of blue sky appeared. We kept turning to look as the storm peeled away from the heavens and the blue sky swelled toward us. So this was Jim Hook's ten-degree drop in temperature! (Later he would tell us that no one had predicted the storm.) The cooling made all the difference in our own hydration. Having guzzled most of a bottle of water after breakfast before dumping out the excess, I hiked now for three hours without taking even a sip from the bladder in my pack, whose sucking tube dangled from my left packstrap.

So efficient was our progress that at 11:30 AM, we stood directly above the 500-foot cliff that led down to our second water cache. I had been trying to keep a log of our mileage as actually hiked. So far, I reckoned, in three and a half days we had rambled some twenty-five miles, gaining fifteen as the crow flies. One-sixth or one-seventh of our total journey. My doubts of the previous days started to dissolve: the Comb should be doable, after all.

At last the sun came out. We sat on the crest, facing west, with our backs to a handy bench, and basked in the warmth as our clothes dried out. Vaughn—for whom, as guide, packaging tasty but lightweight meals was second nature—produced a gourmet lunch: tuna salad wrapped in tortillas, wasabi peas, beef jerky, and gorp. We scarfed down this repast with the appetites of shipwreck survivors.

Through binoculars, we surveyed the Navajo camp below us, the one of which Ramon Redhouse had said, "Nobody there. The folks've probably moved into town." Now there were sheep in the corral, but still no sign of people.

One of us said, "You know, we can maybe just skip that second water cache."

"Let's scout around up here," I suggested. "Check out the potholes."

Leaving our packs at the lunch bench, we set out on separate paths to wander across the slickrock. And all three of us found what we were looking for in abundance: hollows filled to the brim with clear, cool water, the bounty of the violent storm.

Thus all the effort we had undergone to lay that second cache—the trundle up Cane Valley thwarted by the sand dunes, the sixty-mile loop through Monument Valley, the careful hiding of our Rubbermaids behind a boulder as we glanced furtively over our shoulders—had gone for naught. But by skipping the second cache, we saved ourselves hours of strenuous work, scrambling down the 500-foot cliff, filling every bottle we carried, and humping the heavy H_2O back up to the crest. After the trip, Ramon could drive out on an off-day and retrieve the cache, or alert the family who owned the camp where we had placed it, and let them salvage the Rubbermaids and the absurd bottles of store-bought artesian water.

We hoisted our packs and headed on.

Who were we, after all, these three musketeers of the desert, gamboling along the Comb Ridge, and what had brought us together?

I cannot remember the first time I met Greg Child, but it was probably in the 1980s at an annual meeting of the American Alpine Club. Over the years, we had downed the occasional beer together and had shared, in 1994, with our mutual friend Jon Krakauer, one memorable evening of truly drunken tomfoolery. I had never gone climbing with Greg, but I was aware of his stellar accomplishments in the great ranges—not only his ascents of Everest, K2, and the daunting Gasherbrum IV, but bold new routes on such fierce peaks as Trango Tower and Shipton Spire in Pakistan or the Wall of Shadows route on the north face of Mount Hunter in Alaska. Over one of our occasional beers, I mentioned to Greg a trip I had in the back of my head—a circumnavigation of the base of the Simien Plateau in Ethiopia, a marathon hike (with unclimbed towers along the way) that apparently had never been attempted. At once, Greg voiced his enthusiasm. But nothing came of the pipe dream, which, indeed, would have been a logistical tour de force to pull off.

Perhaps I had my guard up a bit. Fourteen years younger than I, Greg was still climbing at top-notch level, while I had long since tapered off. I wasn't sure I wanted to get "sandbagged," as the climbing fraternity dubs the humiliating experience of getting talked onto a route way beyond one's capabilities. My French publisher, Michel Guérin, who was in roughly the kind of climbing shape I maintained, had gone out with Greg for an innocent day's play on a crag in southern France. "Aieee!" Michel had told me over the phone shortly thereafter. "Il est trop fort!" ("He's too strong!")

Meanwhile, I had read a number of the articles Greg had published in climbing journals and found them well wrought and entertaining. In the early 1990s, Greg landed a gig writing a monthly column for *Climbing* magazine. I became a regular reader of these wry, sometimes hilarious, little essays. (Many of these pieces were later collected in Greg's book *Postcards from the Ledge*.) One gem, called "Mother Knows Best," about taking "Mum" out to a local cliff to prove to her that climbing was pretty safe, after all, had me literally weeping with laughter. These deft and often self-deprecating compositions camouflaged the intense perfectionism of Greg's achievements in the mountains.

Born in Sydney, Australia, in 1957, Greg had grown up in a working-class family, his father an office supply wholesaler. As a kid Greg had a geeky affinity for all kinds of reptiles and insects, which he collected and kept as pets. He also started rock climbing at age thirteen, learning his knots out of a Boy Scout handbook, surviving (with his same-age ropemates) the follies of self-taught alpinism. After completing sixth form in public school (the equivalent of senior year of high school in the United States), Greg decided not to go to college. As he would tell me one evening on the Comb, "I couldn't afford it. And I couldn't stand living at home. And if I split from home, I sure as hell wasn't going to be able to go to college."

Instead, at the age of twenty, by now a rabid rock climber, Greg went to Yosemite Valley, where he quickly knocked off three major routes on El Capitan (including the second ascent of the demanding Pacific Ocean Wall). For the next few years, as a climbing bum, he shuttled back and forth between Australia and the United States, until moving here for good in 1980. Meanwhile, to pay the bills he took all kinds of scutwork jobs. As Greg summed up that

Greg Child with daughter, Ariann

period while we were on the Comb, "I was a general laborer. A construction schlepp. A pounder of things with mallets, a digger of holes. They'd hand you a heavy thing and tell you to hit something with it."

Greg settled down in Seattle. In 1981, on Shivling, a proud peak in the Garhwal Himalaya of India, he began a decade and a half crowded with extraordinary new routes on high mountains in the remote ranges. Pairing up with such legends as Doug Scott, as well as with some of the finest alpinists of his own generation, Greg acquired a worldwide reputation. By the mid-1990s he had become a member of the North Face Climbing Team, a sponsored alpinist paid to give slide shows and to test and endorse gear.

Meanwhile, Greg was starting to fulfill a glimmering ambition to make a living as a writer. From getting published in *Climbing* and *Rock and Ice*, he graduated to *Outside* and *National Geographic*. The Mountaineers eventually published three of his books: *Thin Air: Encounters in the Himalaya*, *Mixed Emotions*, and *Postcards from the Ledge*. In 2000 Greg hit the big time, landing a hefty advance for the exclusive story of the four young American climbers who had been literally shot off a big-wall climb in Kyrgyzstan and taken hostage by guerrilla fighters. *Over the Edge*, published in 2002, is a remarkable book, skillfully blending the adventure story of innocents abroad with a savvy analysis of the tragic civil war that had torn asunder that breakaway republic. In the same year, Greg published *Climbing Free*, the as-told-to autobiography of Lynn Hill, arguably the greatest woman climber ever.

In the mid-1990s, Greg moved to Castle Valley, Utah, a tiny hamlet set in a gorgeous basin fifteen miles up the Colorado River from Moab, which had started to become a refuge for rock climbers and other outdoor fanatics (several of Greg's friends already lived there). It was climbing in Utah that turned Greg's fancy toward the Anasazi. As he put it one day in camp, "When you're out on desert rock, you see petroglyphs all the time and the odd cliff dwelling. It got under my skin. The cliff dwelling stuff was an extension of being on the cliffs." Greg's interest was further piqued by reading my 1996 book, *In Search of the Old Ones*, an account of rambling through the backcountry, mostly in southeastern Utah, in quest of obscure ruins and rock art.

Greg and I talked over the phone about getting out in the canyons together, but it was not until the spring of 2002 that we pulled off a brief trip. By then, Greg had pretty much turned his back on big-range mountaineering, but he was rock climbing perhaps better than ever, solid on 5.12, putting up routes here and there that rated a dizzying 5.13. From the start, we took advantage of Greg's technical expertise to get into cliff dwellings and granaries that looked almost impossible to reach, some of which I had first laid covetous eyes on a decade earlier. We also explored canyons neither of us knew, looking for more such ancient wonders.

From the start, we got along well. I was impressed by the fact that this Aussie who had never gone to college was not only a true intellectual, but one of the best-read friends I had ever made. His dry, sharp humor worked the same charm in conversation as it did on the printed page. Starting in 2002, heading into the canyons together every spring and fall, we reached a number of Anasazi sites that we were pretty sure no one else had visited in the last seven centuries since the Anasazi had abandoned their Four Corners heartland. There we made some discoveries so startling that we swore each other to secrecy about the details.

Over campfires, we endlessly debated the "how" of the dazzling Anasazi achievement in the cliffs. My grasp of the archaeology dovetailed with Greg's keen engineering sense of what kinds of prehistoric construction and maneuvering might have been possible. Had the Anasazi used ropes made of yucca? Greg thought yes, I thought no. I contended that if rope had been an Anasazi staple, we'd find remnants of it all through ancient sites. Greg countered that the stuff would have been too precious to leave behind. Even such prolonged debates were exercises in dialectical delight.

A short fellow, about five six, Greg has the strong, wiry build of an expert rock climber. His face, often grizzled with a day or two of stubble, bears the permanent creases of a man who has lived hard. The fixed double parentheses of mouth-framing wrinkles bespeak the skeptic and fatalist I had quickly discerned in Greg. A pair of wire-rim spectacles, however, gives his countenance a touch of the professorial. One of the pleasures of Greg's company is that he is a master of the glib riff, imitating the accents of Europeans with whom he's climbed, or broadening his Aussie twang to deliver some absurdly funny Down-Under soliloquy.

Shortly after first prowling across Cedar Mesa with Greg, I introduced him to Vaughn, with whom I had been pursuing such sport for the previous eight years. Vaughn and I had first met on Cedar Mesa, in fact, in 1994 as I did research (can you call camping and hiking in one of the most beautiful places on Earth "research"?) for *In Search of the Old Ones*. Vaughn and his longtime buddy Fred Blackburn were among the founders of what Fred called the outdoor museum—an alternative to the ethic of the day, which decreed that if you found some unusual artifact in the backcountry, you should report it at once to the Bureau of Land Management (or whatever agency had jurisdiction), so that its archaeologists could recover it and tuck it away safely in some museum. Instead, Fred and Vaughn passionately believed that you should leave the object in place, allowing subsequent wanderers to experience the same thrill you had enjoyed at finding the artifact in

At times the potsherds were so thick on the ground it seemed the earth was fertilized with them. We left every single sherd where we found it.

its aboriginal context. Fred sometimes left a note with the object, as a plea to those future passersby to leave the thing in situ just as he had.

During that week on Cedar Mesa, Fred and Vaughn had cautiously initiated me into the outdoor museum, guiding me to wonderful corners in the canyons where they had made discoveries as long as a decade before, all the while worried that this writer from the East might spill too many beans in print and blow apart the trust on which the museum depended. From the start, however, I subscribed to their purist idealism, eventually titling a chapter in my book "The Outdoor Museum." Writing *In Search of the Old Ones* did not even begin to satisfy my Anasazi itch. During subsequent years, I kept heading back to southeast Utah. I shared several further trips with Fred, but Vaughn was more readily available, and he and I quickly hit it off, just as both of us later would with Greg.

Vaughn was born in 1951 in Grand Island, Nebraska, where his father was a farmer. Eight years later, the family moved to Fort Collins, Colorado. A hippie and self-styled beat poet (he can still quote Gary

Snyder by the yard), Vaughn enrolled at Colorado State University as an anthropology major but dropped out after two years. "School kinda bored me," Vaughn said laconically one evening on the Comb. In his early twenties, he took his own scutwork jobs to pay the bills: ranch hand, construction worker, factory mechanic. The best gig was as a seasonal employee for the Great Western Sugar Company. "It was the perfect job," Vaughn reminisced. "They'd work, then shut down, and I could go backpacking."

Backpacking, indeed! It was during those years that Vaughn and his ascetic buddy pulled off their monthlong, hundred-pound-pack, no-resupply loops in the Beartooths, Sawtooths, and Wind Rivers. Around a campfire one night on Cedar Mesa, Vaughn had Greg and me in stitches as he recounted the end of the Sawtooths trip. Shaggy-maned, coated with grime, four weeks from their last shower, Vaughn and his companion realized they didn't have a single photo of themselves together. Descending toward the roadhead, they saw a fourteen-year-old kid fishing in an alpine lake. They trotted toward the lad, who took one look, sized up a nightmare out of *Deliverance*, dropped his pole, and started running. "No, we just want you to take

Vaughn Hadenfeldt has trudged more miles around Cedar Mesa than most people have had hot dinners.

our picture!" Vaughn yelled, to no avail. In the end, the pair of mountain men trapped the quivering youth in a boulder field at the far end of the lake, handed him the camera, and made him perform his duty.

At CSU Vaughn met Marcia Brody, a fellow student, who he soon realized was his natural soul mate. They were married in 1975. Dessa, their daughter and only child, was born three years later.

Along with his marathon backpacking, Vaughn had also become a rock climber and mountaineer. In Fort Collins in the early 1970s, he had managed a mountaineering store. It seemed logical, then, to go into business himself. In 1978, Vaughn, Marcia, and the infant Dessa moved to Glenwood Springs, Colorado, where they opened Summit Canyon Mountaineering, at the time the only climbing store in that town of six thousand souls, just down the Roaring Fork River from chic, outdoorsy Aspen. The store was soon a rousing success, but Vaughn's wanderlust clashed with the chained-to-the-desk-and-stockroom regimen the business imposed. He climbed regularly in Glenwood Canyon and in the early 1980s served as a guide on a commercial attempt on Denali's South Buttress. ("We three guides could've summitted, but the clients had had enough at 17,000 feet.") Meanwhile, Vaughn had fallen under the spell of the Anasazi after he and a friend backpacked the length of Slickhorn Canyon on Cedar Mesa. More and more through the late 1980s and early 1990s, Vaughn sneaked off from his Glenwood duties to explore Cedar Mesa.

In 1992 Vaughn and Marcia sold the store, and four years later they moved to Bluff. Vaughn had already incorporated himself as Far Out Expeditions, guiding clients on customized trips to the ruins and rock art panels he had discovered over the years. It was a wrenching turnabout for Marcia, who had made many friends in Glenwood, had served on the city council, and loved her job as co-owner of Summit Canyon Mountaineering. Bluff, population three hundred, embedded in Mormon Utah, sixty-five miles from the nearest decent supermarket, had little to offer by way of compensation. In part to make Marcia feel more comfortable, Vaughn and a pair of construction workers built from scratch the beautiful, spacious house they live in today.

With his long, unkempt, dirty-blond hair and his stringy goatee, Vaughn still looks like a hippie crossed, perhaps, with a trapper out of the 1830s. His weather-beaten face is seamed with a network of genial if slightly bemused wrinkles. (All his life, Vaughn has refused to use sunscreen, in part because he hates the greasy feel of the stuff, but mainly because if you wash in a pothole, the scum of oil you leave behind is injurious to the local amphibious life.) Six feet tall and lean, Vaughn camouflages his own intensity behind a laid-back façade. The only time I had ever seen him gain weight was during the year he tried to kick his decades-long habit of tucking a chaw of Skoal under his lower lip. (When Vaughn first started using the stuff, Skoal cost twenty-three cents a tin. Today it retails for over five dollars.) During that year of abstinence, Vaughn also grew uncharacteristically irritable.

Chewing tobacco is one of the two keys to Vaughn's equanimity. The other is that, unlike Greg and me, he has an absolute horror of conflict. In my company, Vaughn had concocted a formula for defusing any disagreement that might start to turn ugly. At such a juncture, he will utter—like some "safe word" in an S&M relationship—the phrase, "How 'bout them Red Sox?"

As I had come to see during those occasions when I tagged along while he guided clients on Cedar Mesa, Vaughn was the finest wilderness guide I had ever known. Even on his own twenty-fifth visit to a ruin, he retained a sense of wonder about the ancients, which he conveyed in thoughtful commentary. No client's question was too dumb to elicit an earnest response.

Over the years, I had wondered what kept Vaughn from succumbing to the kind of burnout I had seen in so many other professional guides. The answer, I thought, was that Vaughn had never lost his exploratory urge. Other guides turn their backyards into pat itineraries, their presentations into canned spiels. But even on that twenty-fifth visit to a familiar ruin, Vaughn always kept his eye out for a new projectile point, for a high granary he had never before noticed. Vis à vis the outdoor museum, he had made some of his most remarkable discoveries with clients in tow.

At the same time, both by temperament and for lack of opportunity, Vaughn had never traveled widely. By 2001, for example, though he probably knew Cedar Mesa better than anyone else alive, Vaughn had never been to Europe. That summer, I talked him into joining me on a quest for the vestiges of an astounding and all-but-forgotten survival story that had befallen four Russian walrus hunters in the eighteenth century, an investigation that would result in a book called *Four Against the Arctic*. I wanted Vaughn along for his friendship, but also because he has the finest eye for artifacts on the ground of anyone I had ever gone into the field with. Vaughn was game for the adventure, even though it cost him several weeks' worth of guiding opportunities. But how many other Americans, I wonder, have ever made their first trip to Europe a junket to Svalbard, the Arctic archipelago far to the north of Norway, between latitudes 76° and 81°? There, for two weeks in late August and early September, we endured frightful weather on the desolate shore of never-inhabited Edgeøya Island, teeming with polar bears, easily the most godforsaken place either of us had ever visited. Vaughn's prowess as a sometime hunter gave me great comfort on the nine separate occasions when we spotted or ran head-on into bears.

My own roundabout journey toward the Comb Ridge had begun, like Greg's, with climbing. In the 1960s and 1970s, between the ages of twenty and thirty-five, I had been obsessed with unclimbed peaks and routes in Alaska. During that decade and a half, I had led or co-led my twelve expeditions to the forty-ninth state, as well as one to the Yukon Territory of subarctic Canada. Alaska was an unexplored and limitless paradise, as far as I was concerned. My whole year revolved around the upcoming summer's campaign in the Far North.

Meanwhile I had graduated from Harvard in mathematics, gone to the University of Denver for grad school in English, earned a PhD

David Roberts sweating out near-century temperatures on the Comb

in five years, and started teaching at Hampshire College in western Massachusetts. All the while, I wanted to "be" a writer. The lucky success of getting my first two books—each an account of one of my Alaskan expeditions—published when I was still in my mid-twenties fooled me into thinking that I could teach for a living and write productively in my spare time. During nine years at Hampshire, I fell victim to my own burnout. Not until I was thirty-six years old did I dare to quit teaching and try to make a living as a freelance writer. Today, I regard those fourteen years in academe as a mistake, a long detour that kept me off my chosen path.

By that point, in 1979, I had pretty much turned my back on big-range mountaineering. Alaska, sadly, no longer gleamed in my unconscious as the land of limitless hope and ambition. During my first years as a freelancer, I was able to sample all kinds of non-mountaineering adventures—a partial first descent of a river in New Guinea, an excursion into subtropical Australia in quest of undiscovered aboriginal rock art, a jaunt into the Sierra Madre of northern Mexico in the footsteps of Geronimo, and the like. But for a solid decade, I could find no personal quest to replace the siren call that unclimbed Alaskan mountains had once sung for me.

Then, one day in 1987, I embarked on a mere three-day backpack into Bullet Canyon, a tributary of Grand Gulch on Cedar Mesa. As a kid, I had visited many of the national parks and monuments of the Southwest that are devoted to prehistoric cultures: Mesa Verde, Chaco Canyon, Wupatki, Montezuma's Castle, and the like. Yet I gleaned from those outings little more than a dull, museum-like admiration for the long-vanished builders.

At Perfect Kiva and Jailhouse ruins in Bullet Canyon, to my astonished delight, I found potsherds and corncobs still strewn in the dirt, where they had lain for more than seven centuries. I camped beside the same spring that had watered the ancients. And for three days, I ran into no other hikers in that sovereign canyon. The Anasazi hook was set.

Writing *In Search of the Old Ones* only intensified my fascination with the prehistoric Southwest. By 2004 there was no happier way anywhere in the world for me to spend a day or a week than to set out down a canyon new to me with a congenial comrade, as we searched for signs of the Old Ones. And by then, no comrades were more congenial than Greg and Vaughn.

Comradely though our canyon play together was, however, we each freely acknowledged that it was a fiercely competitive business. As I had seen—not only on our third day of the Comb Ridge hike when Greg had found our first projectile point, but on numerous previous occasions—it drove Vaughn crazy if someone else spotted an artifact or a petroglyph before he did. During our first hikes together on Cedar Mesa, with Greg still in his Anasazi apprenticeship, Vaughn and I had to grant that he had an excellent natural eye. But he was also a bit overeager, and we mercilessly teased him about what we called his "false positives"—a natural pattern of fracture lines on some distant cliff that Greg mistook for rock art, a tumble of roof-fall stones inside some alcove that had tricked him into seeing a masoned wall.

The competitiveness was good-natured but keen. Because of his guiding duties, Vaughn had to pass up some of Greg's and my prowls on Cedar Mesa. Sometimes, on returning to Vaughn's house after an eight-hour hike, Greg and I would be greeted with the query, "You guys find anything cool?"

"Nah," Greg would answer. "Just some beat-up old granaries."

"Good!" Vaughn would chortle.

For my part, in the depths of a snowbound January or February in my home in Cambridge, Massachusetts, I would often seethe with envy of Greg's and Vaughn's daily chance to hop into the car, drive an hour toward some unnamed canyon, and set out on a fresh quest. I even toyed with the idea of moving to the Southwest, only to come to the conclusion that I was an incurable urbanite, addicted to world-class libraries and bookstores and to restaurants serving exotic cuisine. Tucson or Salt Lake City or Denver would not do it for me, and I knew that I would go off the deep end trying to live in a town like Bluff or Castle Valley.

A piquant manifestation of our rivalry came one week in the spring of 2004. Tipped off by an old-timer from Mexican Hat who remembered stumbling, some twenty years before, across a beautifully preserved kiva with an intact ladder in a particular side-canyon, Greg and Vaughn set out, armed with a good description from the fellow himself, to find this backcountry prodigy. Instead, they spent a marathon day discovering virtually nothing. A few days later, Greg drove solo back down to Cedar Mesa from Castle Valley to poke into the next side-canyon north of his and Vaughn's long ramble. At the end of another fruitless day, as he returned to his vehicle, Greg spotted Vaughn's truck parked a few hundred yards away. He left a note under Vaughn's windshield wiper: "Go home. No kivas here."

As we set out on the Comb Ridge on September 1, Greg was forty-seven years old, Vaughn fifty-three, and I the graybeard at sixty-one. During the previous two and a half years, in all the possible permutations, the three of us had spent weeks in the backcountry, getting along famously, with hardly a cross word during even the most trying of times. The Comb Ridge, however, would test our friendship in ways we had never before experienced.

⁂

On September 4, having decided that we could skip the second water cache, we plugged onward right on the crest of the Comb. The storm that we thought had cleared out, however, regathered itself and struck again. To the south, we saw huge thunderclouds massing. A stiff south wind shoved these cumulonimbus giants toward us. The sun disappeared. By 2:30 in the afternoon, it was sprinkling again, while lightning forked the sky about ten miles off the Comb.

We rounded a tall sandstone arête—yet another of the Comb's teeth—and abruptly entered a miniature basin tucked just below the crest on the west. This "hanging garden," as I would come to think of it, looked like the perfect campsite. The tooth itself served as a windbreak, in the northern lee of which we might pitch our tents, out of the brunt of the gale. There were dead junipers strewn about the basin, promising abundant firewood. There were several big potholes full of rainwater. We had been hiking for six hours, covering about seven miles, but to stop here would mean calling it a day at 3:00 PM. Still, I thought, we were in no rush, we had saved maybe three or four hours of toil by skipping the water cache, and we were unlikely to find a better camping spot. I said so to my colleagues.

"We gotta find an alcove," Vaughn rejoined, without even breaking stride. Ever since the rain had started falling, Vaughn's *idée fixe* had been to hole up in the shelter of an overhanging cliff—an alcove of the sort the Anasazi had chosen for their cliff dwellings. In just such aeries, he had spent many a snug night waiting out storms in the Southwest. The trouble was, for the last ten miles or so the Comb had been notably deficient in alcoves. Across that stretch, in fact, we had seen fewer signs of the ancients than on any section of the ridge so far.

There was nothing to do now but tag along in the wake of Vaughn's headlong march, as Greg and I had done all day. I felt vexed, however, by such a process of decision making. As I wrote that evening in my diary, "Vaughn just charges on. I get irritated that we don't discuss the decision. Greg says it doesn't matter to him. He'd be inclined just to push on until dark. (I'm slightly the tiredest of the 3 of us, so more inclined to quit early.)"

We hiked on for another half mile, finding nothing that faintly resembled an alcove. At last I demanded a halt and a discussion. We threw our packs down and started arguing. "We're not going to find an alcove," I insisted. "I vote for back there." I pointed south, toward the hanging garden I had fallen in love with. Greg muttered a curse under his breath and headed off to the east, apparently to scout for a sheltered site lower on the Comb.

After ten minutes of haggling between Vaughn and me, with most of the verbiage issuing from my mouth, he suddenly exclaimed, "All right, let's do it!" He seized his pack, wrenched it onto his back, and started retracing his steps at the same impetuous pace he had maintained all day.

Hoisting my own pack, scrambling to catch up, I said, "You don't have to get pissed off."

"I'm not pissed off!" answered Vaughn. Meanwhile, Greg was out of sight to the east. If he returned to his pack and found us absent, I reasoned, he wouldn't know whether we'd gone forward or backward. I said as much to Vaughn. He didn't answer, plowing ahead in his stolid funk. So I stopped and waited for Greg, who came back into sight after another fifteen minutes.

It was the closest thing to a spat that we had yet endured on the Comb, and, to my dismay, it lingered on after we regained the hanging garden. Ostentatiously, as if to demonstrate the virtues of the windbreak, I set up my tent directly under the north wall of the high tooth. But meanwhile the lightning was coming closer, and the rain had picked up. Vaughn declared the garden too dangerous for a campsite. He scrambled over some giant boulders and two bands of slickrock, dropping about a hundred feet down the west side of the crest. I found him hunkering in the marginal shelter not of a true alcove, but of a cliff that overhung by perhaps five degrees, allowing us barely to get out of the rain. We sat for a while in silence.

"You don't want to camp here, do you?" I asked.

"Sure. Better'n up there." He tilted his head toward my hanging garden, out of sight above.

"God, this looks miserable. There's hardly any level ground to pitch a tent."

"You can camp where you want. Let's cook down here."

As I had long recognized, Vaughn and I were both pretty stubborn fellows. But on our hikes on Cedar Mesa, we had never locked horns in an impasse like this one. For the next hour, we faced the prospect of a divided camp, Vaughn spending the night on his scruffy little ledge, I sleeping in the hanging garden, exposed to lightning. Greg had not yet made up his mind where to bivouac.

Now the storm passed over us in a dramatic, fast-moving display of aerial pyrotechnics. In its wake, Monument Valley to the west turned a hazy orange, as a violent rain- and dust-storm wreaked its havoc. As the clouds cleared to the north, we saw an eerie swath of white stretching for perhaps ten miles across the floor of the badlands between Monument Valley and the San Juan River. "My god," I said. "That's gotta be hail."

Vaughn peered through his binoculars. "Yeah," he said finally. "It's hail."

"And look at the Abajos." For the first time during our traverse, we could see all the way to the high though diminutive mountain range that rose west of Monticello, Utah. The Abajos actually lay beyond the end of our hike, where at last the Comb Ridge dwindled into nothingness. "Isn't that new snow?"

The weather itself, some of the most spectacular any of us had seen in the Southwest, rubbed a kind of healing balm into our frayed nerves. By dusk, the sky was clear. Vaughn relented and agreed to pitch his tent up in my hanging garden. We built a fire and sat around it, staring into the flames, luxuriating in the heat as the temperature dropped below forty degrees Fahrenheit. It would be the only campfire we would indulge in during the whole traverse.

I stayed up later than Greg and Vaughn, watching the fire burn down, relishing that special moment when the last blue flame flickered out and the coals pulsed gray and dull red. The sky was ablaze with stars, the constellations Lyra and Cygnus directly overhead, Gemini climbing over the eastern horizon. Saturn hung high in the western sky, an adamantine point of white.

At last I crawled into my sleeping bag but continued to watch the sky through the netting of the tent roof. In the wake of our flare-up, I felt a deep contentment. There was nothing I would rather do than camp here, no friends with whom I would more gladly share such beauty than Greg and Vaughn. But that day would not be the last time on the Comb that simply trying to decide where to spend the night would rub our feelings raw.

⦿⦿⦿

Just before sunrise, I heard an owl hooting nearby. I rose to see Venus in the east, brilliant yellow, far brighter than any star. The afternoon before, we had noticed that the hanging garden was strewn with pot-sherds and lithics. So the Anasazi had agreed with me, I mused smugly, that this was a good place to camp. Now, before the others arose, I walked in aimless loops across the small basin, stooped over to spy the prettier flakes and sherds.

Troubled perhaps by our near quarrel, Vaughn, who seldom re-membered his dreams, had woken from the grips of a nightmare. Over a breakfast of Cream of Wheat laced with dates and pine nuts, coffee, and Crystal Lite peach tea, he recounted it to us. "There was just the two of us on the Comb," he said, nodding at me. "We come down to the San Juan, it's in flood like the Grand Canyon. I jump in; I'm slammed from rock to rock. You're waiting back on the shore. Finally I crawl out of the river and up to this house."

Vaughn stirred the Cream of Wheat. "A woman comes to the door. 'My friend, I think he's dead,' I say. She opens the garage door. There's a big, old, giant Army truck, lots of cracked tires. She's pluggin' in a battery charger. I say, 'Shouldn't we call Bluff?' She leaves. Then Dad and the young 'uns show up. He's holding a double-bit ax with a broken handle. At first I think they're bein' friendly. But he's about to cleave my forehead with it. The kids are all surrounding me. I grab hold of the handle—and then I wake up."

Our mood this morning had shifted 180 degrees from the tensions of the previous afternoon. Scouting for potsherds, I had discovered a white moth, its wings impaled on a prickly pear spine. Now I showed it to Greg, the erstwhile teenage entomologist. I had assumed the moth was dead, but it stirred when Greg gently touched it. "Wow," he said. "Must've been the storm. How else would a bug get stuck on a prickly pear?"

Greg got out his macro lens and shot off a series of portraits. Then he extricated the wings from the spine. The moth fluttered feebly. "He looks fucked," said Greg.

"You know the great Robert Frost poem, 'Design'?" I asked. Greg shook his head. "White spider, white moth, white flower. It's about evil," I pontificated, and then quoted the closing couplet, "'What but design of darkness to appall?—If design govern in a thing so small?'"

Greg wasn't too interested in my English class. He poked at the moth with a twig, until it managed to recover, crawl through the weeds, and at last rise into uncertain flight. We got to our feet. Greg was grinning over his rescue mission. "That's cool. See, in 'real life,'" he said, wiggling his fingers to mime quotation marks, "you'd never have time to stand around and look at a moth."

We set off, rejuvenated, into the fresh, cool morning. In the first mile, we passed three old Navajo sweat lodges, sagging pyramids of hewn branches standing less than three feet off the ground. As we paused before one, Vaughn nudged a small pile of rocks with his toe. "Those are the heating stones," he said.

"It's funny," he went on. "Usually you find sweat lodges associated with hogans. But up here, they're probably for the sheepherders."

"Is it all about curing illness?" I asked.

"Unh-uh. It's about just feelin' good. Gettin' clean. Sweat it all out. They're always done with rituals, though."

A little farther along the ridge, we came in sight of a lonely hogan, 700 feet below us to the west and about two miles away. It stood in the morning shadow of the Comb, a curl of smoke issuing from the chimney. The sight occasioned an impromptu debate among the three of us. I had always been struck by the preference of Navajos on the reservation for living in isolation from one another, one family and hogan set far apart from all the ones scattered around it. As we had driven back roads to lay our second water cache, I had been further struck by the fact that, only ten miles from the hogan in which Ramon Redhouse had grown up, he didn't know the names of the traditional Navajo families living along certain stretches of Cane Valley.

Was the Navajo penchant for isolation intrinsic to the very culture? Greg and I thought so, but Vaughn demurred. "It could be about sheepherding," he offered, son as he was of a Nebraska farmer. "Think how much water and graze sheep need."

"We ought to look this up," I said.

"Where?"

I had always been far more keenly interested in the Anasazi than in their successors, the Navajo. But in the months before our trip, I had done a lot of reading about the Athapaskans from the north, as I would continue to do during our journey. In terms of Navajo perceptions of the Comb, there seemed to be some fundamental puzzles.

The only work in which I could find any real discussion of that Navajo take on the Comb was McPherson's *Sacred Land, Sacred View*. Ramon Redhouse had told us that the Diné name for the long ridge was Saba'naha, Gray or Tan Ridge. McPherson's informants, however, had insisted that the name for the Comb was Tse'k'ann, or Rocks Standing Up. Different elders had emphasized different aspects of the mythic significance of the Comb, in a congeries of values and images that seemed mutually contradictory to my Western mind, but which probably did not confound the Diné who lived in sight of the great ridge.

Thus, according to McPherson, the Comb Ridge was at once the spine of the Earth itself made visible, the rest of it circling the globe; one of four giant arrowheads protecting the Navajo world; a Big Snake, its tail pointing toward Kayenta, and thus associated with witchcraft; and a furrow dug with the knife of Wind as he cut up the body of Changing Bear Maiden.

Navajos, I knew, view features in the landscape not only as playing critical roles in mythic narratives, but as being imbued with powerful innate capacities for good or for evil. McPherson further alludes to the Comb Ridge as being a battle site of the Hero Twins, the supernatural beings who, by slaying one monster after another, made the world safe for the people. All such sites have a strong positive aura for the people. Most intriguingly, McPherson found that during the turbulent 1860s, when an American army force led by Kit Carson and employing Ute mercenaries hunted down thousands of Navajo "renegades" to send them on the Long Walk to their doleful concentration camp at Bosque Redondo in eastern New Mexico, the Comb came to be seen as a critical dividing line. All land west of the Comb was Navajo, and good. All land east of the ridge was the province of the enemy.

An important question is when the Navajo first lived on and around the Comb. The people may say they have lived since time immemorial within the quadrangle formed by the four sacred mountains. The most liberal anthropologists might grant a first appearance of these Athapaskans in the Southwest as early as the fourteenth century. But there is considerable reason to believe that the Navajo did not begin to inhabit such regions as Monument Valley, Navajo Mountain, and the Comb Ridge until the nineteenth century, and perhaps even as late as the 1860s. (Kit Carson's notorious roundup may have been the force that drove them into these refuges.)

The region in the Southwest where, according to agnostic archaeologists, the Navajo first unmistakably appear is the shallow canyons tributary to the San Juan on the south, some thirty miles southeast of present-day Aztec, New Mexico—canyons such as Largo, Gobernador, Carrizo, and Blanco. Collectively, this region is known as Dinétah. It was not until the 1770s that Dinétah was abandoned, perhaps under the pressure of Ute and Comanche raids, and only after that date do the Navajo first show up in the Lukachukai Mountains and Canyon de Chelly in northeast Arizona. These new homelands still lie some distance to the southeast of Comb Ridge. Carson's troops raided Canyon de Chelly in 1863–64, cutting down the Diné's precious peach trees, taking many prisoners, and driving many others to flight. Perhaps it was only then that Navajo refugees flocked to such places as the Comb Ridge. Almost no archaeology has been done on the Comb, and as far as I know, none of it has focused on the Navajo. So the question of when the newcomers first built their hogans on and around the Comb remains unsolved. If that advent came as late as the 1860s, it seems extraordinary that in a little more than a century (McPherson's interviews having taken place in the 1980s) the long ridge could have been woven so inextricably into the very creation myth of the people.

A week later during our backpack trip, I would gain a more intimate Diné insight into the Comb Ridge, in the pages of a book called *The Journey of Navajo Oshley*. Born sometime between 1879 and 1893, Oshley had been a sheepherder and medicine man who led a hard life in northern Arizona and southern Utah, finally coming to rest in a "half house" in which he whiled out his last years in the town of Blanding. Winston Hurst, a friend of Vaughn's and mine who had become one of the leading archaeologists in this part of the Southwest, had grown up in Blanding. One of his schoolmates was a son of Navajo Oshley. In 1978, as fodder for his master's thesis at Eastern New Mexico University, Winston had interviewed the old-timer. The sessions—fourteen of them in all—were tape recorded. Since Winston did not speak Navajo and Oshley only a few words of English, the old man's son had sat in and offered regular synopses of his father's stories.

Winston sent the tapes to the Utah State Historical Society, where they sat untranslated for a decade. Yet he knew that those interviews were an ethnographic gold mine, and he tipped off his friend and fellow Blandingite Robert S. McPherson to their existence. In 1988 McPherson had the tapes transcribed and translated, and then wove them into the autobiographical narrative he finally published in 2000. Sadly, Oshley himself died shortly after the translating was begun.

Oshley grew up at a place the Navajo called Sitting Red Rock, just south of the Comb Ridge and very near where we had commenced our hike on September 1. His mother was from Cane Valley—the same shallow wash on which we looked down from our hike on September 3, 4, and 5 and where we had placed our second water cache. Oshley remembered that his mother had raised corn, melons, and squash in Cane Valley, wrapping her produce in tree bark and burying it in storage pits in the sand dunes to preserve it. (So the sand dunes that had thwarted Vaughn's truck on August 30 were good for something!)

Though he did not identify its location, Oshley said that in his youth, the nearest trading post was a three- to four-day round-trip journey from home. Later in his childhood the family moved to Cane Valley and built a hogan very close to where, more than a century later, we would leave that second water cache. The Comb was a playground for the boy and his cousins. As the old-timer remembered in 1978, "We took big flat rocks for sleds and slid down the rock slopes, which was a lot of fun." On one such ride, however, Oshley nearly killed himself, when he slipped off his sled and watched the heavy stone fly over his careening body.

Near this second home, Anglo prospectors had blasted a diagonal trail up the steep west face of the Comb. This primitive track was known to the Navajo as Where Dynamite Made a Road. Oshley remembered burros carrying loads of melons and squash down "that awful trail, and if they slipped, they fell off and died." (Placing our water cache, we had found the lower end of that diagonal thoroughfare, now a mere rut in the hillside. Nonetheless, we would have hiked down the old road in preference to the scrambling route I had scouted the previous spring, had we actually retrieved our cache.)

During his decades of herding along the Comb, Oshley gained an exquisite knowledge not only of its reliable springs, but of which potholes and tanks were most likely to hold water for days after a rainstorm. He frequently advised others who set off to cross the Comb just where they could find water and firewood. (What we wouldn't have given to have tapped into the old-timer's fund of water lore!)

All his life, Oshley observed a scrupulous caution with regard to things Anasazi. Unlike other Navajos, he never picked up the arrowheads he found lying on the ground. One passage in the book, in particular, resonated for me. In the testimony of the old-timer's good friend John Holiday, a Navajo shaman interviewed in 1999, who forms an invaluable second source for McPherson's *Journey*, "Oshley used to protect himself from the influence of the Anasazi. He used boiled juniper tree's juice, which he applied all over his body during a sweat hogan ceremony. Doing this ritual helped to cure his mind and any ill feelings that might be around the Anasazi dwellings." To think that, sometime early in the twentieth century, Oshley might have purified himself thus in one of the same sagging sweat lodges we had found on September 5 gave me the most tangible connection to the Navajo past that I would make during our whole trek.

During his lifetime, Oshley evidently crossed the Comb Ridge hundreds of times. No Navajo could have known the place better than he. Yet in his narrative, Oshley seems never to have felt entirely comfortable on the Comb. On those occasions when he was forced to camp on or near the crest, he always passed an uneasy night, alert to strange sounds, or to the absence of normal ones. For Navajo Oshley, there was always something spooky about the long ridge, some malevolent aura that he never quite articulated—for such things, to a traditional Navajo, are best left unspoken.

There was no question by now: we were in good shape after five days without a beer, five days of lugging heavy burdens across the endless ups and downs of the Comb. On September 5 we made our best time yet, as the ridge uncharacteristically leveled off for miles at a stretch. We cruised along a flat bench just west of the crest. One mile of that bench, I thought, was the most serenely beautiful stretch of Comb we had yet traversed—a rosy bedrock plateau spangled with potholes full of rainwater.

When we had started our journey, the towers of Monument Valley had risen straight north of us. The nearest big landmark, also to the north, was the black volcanic plug of Agathla (the "wool twiner" held by a giant mythic woman embedded in the very landscape; also one of the "sky pillars" that holds up the firmament). Now, only five days later, Agathla had dwindled to a distant cone far to the southwest, and Monument Valley was fast receding on the west. The day before, we had rounded the outlying cliff and pinnacle—Meridian Butte and Rooster Rock—that separate the Comb from the famous valley of the John Ford westerns. Glancing over my left shoulder at these landmarks, I felt a giddy elation at having covered so much ground.

My only problem was that I had developed a sharp, painful stitch in my left shoulder. No adjustment of pack straps could relieve the agony of that dagger in the muscle. Twice, at rest stops, Greg massaged my sore shoulder. The treatment worked for about an hour before the stitch needled back into my consciousness. In the midst of such smooth sailing across clean slickrock on a perfect sunny day, that nagging pain was a true annoyance.

At lunch, I pulled out the map, the Garnet Ridge 1:24,000 quadrangle we were winging across (we had already left four other quadrangles in the dust). There was no doubt about it: we were making better progress than we had dared hope. This very afternoon, we would, in fact, easily reach our third water cache, the one under the big juniper not far from Chester and Rena Benally's house.

One of the good-natured but spirited disagreements that had waxed and waned over the course of our three-year collaboration in the canyonlands had to do with that handy gadget the Global Positioning System. Vaughn and I had sworn that we would never resort to a GPS to locate ourselves in the landscape. Using a GPS was cheating. Already the doodads, we had noticed, had unleashed a new breed of "bozos" into the backcountry, hikers who could read neither a map nor the terrain under their feet. Vaughn refused to let his clients carry GPSs, and he and I had led a campaign that successfully persuaded a Utah publisher to drop GPS coordinates to Anasazi ruins and rock art from an upcoming guidebook to—among other sacred places—Cedar Mesa.

To Greg, Vaughn's and my idealism was pure Luddite sentimentality. He himself was an unconflicted user of the GPS. Though we had threatened to break or accidentally misplace Greg's toy, Vaughn and I had grudgingly allowed him to bring it along on the Comb. On August 30, as we had taped up our Rubbermaids for the third and last water cache, Vaughn and I had peered intensely at surrounding land-marks, had tried to memorize the shape of the one big juniper among scores of junipers halfway up the nondescript east slope of the Comb. Greg, meanwhile, had simply plugged the coordinates into his GPS.

Now, at our third break, shortly before 3:00 PM, I scrutinized the map. "The cache is about a quarter mile from here," I announced.

Greg had his gadget out. "Three-tenths of a mile, to be exact," he smirked.

Had the potholes full of water that we had sailed past in the morning persisted, we might well have skipped our third cache, as we had our second. But during the last mile or two, the bedrock had turned to dirt and sand. We hadn't found a single water pocket during that stretch. We needed the third cache, after all.

We stopped just below the crest of the Comb, directly above the cache, which lay, we thought, only a couple of hundred yards away. Once more, I insisted on a discussion. Should we pitch camp up here first, and then retrieve the cache, or get the cache first and then decide where to camp? This time it was Greg who lost his patience. "While you guys are going over all these permutations," he spat, "we could have the thing by now." He jumped to his feet and started hiking fast down the eastern slope. Vaughn said, "I'm going, too." Before he left, he tied his red jacket to a bush to mark the spot where he and Greg had left their backpacks.

Feeling like a kid kicked out of the neighborhood tree house, I sheepishly trudged back to the crest to scout a place to pitch our tents. As I threw down my pack, I heard the sudden noise of hoof beats. I turned to look south and saw three sleek black horses galloping across a distant shelf. Could they be wild, I wondered? Before I could get out my binoculars to look for brands, they were out of sight.

Vaughn and Greg were back in half an hour, each lugging a pair of two-and-a-half-gallon bottles of artesian water. "Thanks, guys," I said, relieving Greg of one of his bottles. (It was only much later that Vaughn, competitive to the end, told me how gratifying it was that Greg, guided by his GPS, had veered off in the wrong direction. It was Vaughn's dead reckoning, after all, that had relocated the cache.)

I mentioned the horses. "Might've been wild," I added.

Vaughn snorted. "There's no wild horses around here."

"How do you know?"

Vaughn didn't answer.

On the crest of the ridge, I had found a geologic anomaly that would furnish us with the most perfect campsite of all the ones we would occupy on the Comb. Here, a slickrock shelf was festooned with five gigantic potholes, each far deeper than a man is tall. The floor of the deepest sat fully thirty feet below the rim. Its walls overhung on all sides, making the pit a natural trap; but Greg was able to shinny down a tree growing out of the depths. On the floor of this bell-shaped cavern he found a lot of Anasazi lithics, many small animal bones, and two black-on-orange potsherds. Another pothole, fifteen feet deep, had a cottonwood growing out of its center—the only specimen of that deciduous, stream-loving tree we would find along the hundred miles of the Comb's crest. A cottonwood seed, we guessed, must have been blown by a tempest all the way up here from some distant wash, and here it had sprung roots in the thin soil at the bottom of the pit. The tree had flourished in this unlikely spot because the pothole protected it from competing vegetation, while guaranteeing a regular flow of rainwater.

Two of the pits were in fact full of water now. So we could have done without the cache after all. Most beguilingly, leading into one of the giant tanks, I found an old Anasazi hand-and-toe trail of some six or seven steps. The pit had served as a walk-in well for the ancients!

Vaughn and Greg may have preferred to keep backpacking till sundown, but I was heartily in favor of early quitting times for our days' marches. To me, some of the best hours we spent on the Comb were those between setting up camp and sunset, when we could wander packless about our surroundings and make small discoveries. Here, the Comb plunged westward not in its usual uniform precipice, but in a cascade of purple domes, the petrified ghosts of former sand dunes. Wandering among several of these, I found potsherds everywhere, many of them black-on-white and black-on-red. Off on a different tack, Greg and Vaughn scared up a gray fox, the only one we would see on our hike. Then, as the cliff at last shelved toward the vertical, they found a staircase of Anasazi foot- and handholds. Greg climbed two-thirds of the way down the exposed, hundred-foot staircase, finding an old metal cable strung along the lowest and steepest stretch. The staircase, obviously, had given the Old Ones access to the precious giant tanks on the crest, and centuries later, Navajos had improved the route with the cable.

Thanks to our smooth progress, we were now a full day ahead

of our anticipated schedule. Tomorrow, September 6, we would easily reach the dirt road that crossed the Comb, linking Highway 163 west of Mexican Hat with Highway 160 west of Mexican Water—a twenty-five-mile-long shortcut that furnished the Navajo their only vehicular transect of the Comb on the reservation. At that road's summit pass, we had scheduled our second rendezvous and resupply with Jim Hook—but for 2:00 PM on September 7.

Now I pulled an item out of my pack that we had carried for thirty-six miles without using it once—an object about which I harbored a generous load of ambivalence. Planning the trip months before, we had finally agreed to take along a satellite phone. Cell phones don't work on the reservation segment of the Comb: if we wanted to have outside contact, it was a sat phone or nothing. We rationalized the decision as a safety factor, in case someone got injured; but we knew beforehand that the most likely use for the phone would be to revise our logistics, as we wished to do now.

In our younger days, all three of us had gone off for more than a month at a time into true wilderness—the Alaska Range or the Karakoram—without any hope of phone or radio contact to the outside world. On my Alaskan expeditions, I had learned to luxuriate in the absolute frontier between "in" and "out" that flying or hiking in to some remote glacier imposed on my life. With no hope of rescue, one developed not constant anxiety but a life-asserting sense of utter self-reliance.

Shortly before the trip, I had read Ted Kerasote's small, trenchant book, *Out There: In the Wild in a Wired Age*, a memoir about a two-man canoe trip on the Horton River in Arctic Canada that had been profoundly transformed by Kerasote's buddy's insistence on taking along a sat phone to stay in frequent touch with his wife back in Jackson Hole, Wyoming. Perhaps Greg, Vaughn, and I had all three turned soft in middle age, but we finally agreed that the sat phone would be a welcome crutch on our long backpack. At a not inconsiderable expense ($250 plus shipping and phone call charges), we rented a device from an outfit in Florida.

We had agreed—unlike Kerasote's companion, who from the wilds of the Horton had chatted fulsomely and almost daily not only with his wife, but with his family and his law office—to limit our own calls to the strictly necessary. Vaughn hoped never to speak into the damned contraption, leaving all the phoning up to me.

Now, just before dinner, I took out the sat phone and dialed Recapture Lodge. Jim Hook's voice answered as clearly as if he were just a few blocks away in Bluff. He was happy to change the schedule—he'd meet us at 2:00 PM tomorrow, not the day after.

I hung up, then looked at my companions. "Does that feel like cheating, or what?"

Greg had his know-it-all smirk on his face. "What's the difference between that and a GPS?" he taunted.

We were off in the morning by 8:30. The freshening benediction of the storm had expired: now the temperature was back in the 90s, and the fierce sun was sucking the moisture out of the potholes as we hiked. In light tee shirts and shorts, we sweated like pigs. Again, the going was easier than we dared hope. "Do you realize," Greg said, as the roadcut came into view, "that in six days we haven't seen a single footprint?"

We got to the road three hours early, at 11:00 AM. At Vaughn's suggestion, we clambered down into a small ravine, where we could sprawl in the shade of several junipers. From this lair, we could hear the occasional car pass by thirty feet above our heads, but we were out of sight of any drivers or passengers.

From the start of our trip, Vaughn and I had aired our different feelings about Navajo contact on the rez. In what seemed to me a slightly paranoid fashion, he voiced his fears about running into vicious Navajo dogs or hostile Navajos who might question our intrusion. "I just don't want to be seen," he said more than once on our hike. Greg was inclined to agree. Thus our holing up in the ravine was a matter of hiding as much as seeking shade.

I felt quite the opposite—that encounters with traditional Navajos such as the Benallys would enrich, not endanger, our trip. Although Vaughn had spent far more time than I on Cedar Mesa, I had a leg up on him here, in that I had done quite a bit more hiking than he on the reservation. (Greg had explored almost not all in Navajo country.) Always armed with a permit from Window Rock, I had backpacked for as long as eight days at a time, sometimes solo, among the canyons of the Tsegi and the Lukachukais, the Rainbow Plateau, and elsewhere. Perhaps four or five times, I had been asked by a Navajo whom

I ran into in the backcountry to show my permit, but not one of those meetings had turned unpleasant. Friends of Vaughn's and mine had indeed recounted the occasional episode in which local Navajos (usually young guys) had turned threatening. But I was convinced that the only really dangerous encounters on the rez were likely to occur in such tourist-thronged precincts as Canyon de Chelly National Monument, where poverty and unemployment had conspired with booze and drugs to turn part of a generation of adolescents and young men into occasional thieves and even assailants.

Was Vaughn's aversion simply a kind of cultural squeamishness, a discomfort with alien people? Was that why we were hiding below the roadbed rather than sitting beside our packs and waving at the cars that went by as we waited for Jim's resupply? Yet even as I nursed my self-righteous critique, I recognized that there were two sides to the coin. Perhaps Vaughn viewed my openness to the Navajo as simply naïve. One angry faceoff with a gun-toting Navajo who ordered us off his land, permit or no stinking permit, could sabotage our whole trip.

In my own meditative funk, I volunteered now to hike ahead a mile or two and scout water holes while Greg and Vaughn waited for Jim. What I found might dictate how much water we would have to carry from the resupply. In the last four miles before the roadcut, we had found not a drop of pothole water. In this withering heat, would we once again be forced to load up twelve quarts apiece, twenty-four miserable pounds of aqua straight out of the tap in Bluff?

Hiking fast with only a day pack and a couple of water bottles, I climbed three hundred feet toward a handsome scattering of squat orange towers. To do so, I had to skirt one of the few Navajo homesteads we would find near the crest of the Comb, as opposed to on the lowlands on either side. Through my binoculars, I observed a trailer and a collection of pickups, both derelict and operative. I heard dogs barking but saw nobody.

In just over an hour I completed a three-mile loop toward the north. In all that distance, I found only a single pothole with some five or six gallons of water in it, on a saddle between two graceful domes, at an altitude of 5500 feet. Every other pothole was bone dry. Yet that one miniature reservoir in the bedrock meant all the difference to our plans. I returned to tell Vaughn and Greg the good news. Then, waiting in the ravine, huddled in juniper shade, I perused the Mexican Hat SE quadrangle onto which we had intruded. A small lightbulb

Water pockets like this one, just a few inches deep, and siphoned into our bottles through a decontaminating filter, could keep us going for days.

flashed in my brain. "Hey, guys, guess what?" I said. "Sometime this morning, we crossed the border from Arizona into Utah, without even realizing it."

The road looming just above our heads, Ramon Redhouse had informed us, had been a Navajo trail long before automobiles came to the reservation. In Vaughn's truck on August 30, as we had turned the corner in Cane Valley, only two miles west of here, Ramon, who had grown up nearby, had pointed up at the pass and remembered, "When I was a child, my grandmother was in her nineties. She told me her father took her by horseback over that trail to go to boarding school in Shiprock. Took two days—one day to Teec Nos Pos—they'd camp under a cottonwood tree there—then another day to Shiprock."

As usual, Jim Hook was right on time. I seized the sports section of the *USA Today* that I had beseeched Jim to bring to each resupply. The Red Sox were two and a half games behind the Yankees with less than a month to play. Close, but probably not close enough. The all-too-familiar fall scenario was playing itself out once more. Even on Comb Ridge, the Curse of the Bambino was alive and well.

Now Jim told us the shocking news from the "real" world—about the massacre in the Russian school at Beslan of some 340 hostages, half of them children. I thought of the four children of his own, whom Jim adored, as I watched his usually cheery face twist with anguish while he recounted the Chechen onslaught, which had happened just the day before.

It took us more than an hour to sort out our gear and food and re-load our packs. We discussed the unexpected storm of September 4. "It rained three-quarters of an inch in Bluff," said Jim. "And the San Juan got up to 13,000 cfs." I whistled. The river's normal flow this time of year was something like a mere 500 to 600 cubic feet per second.

Less than a week hence, Jim would bring small inflatable rafts—"rubber duckies," he called them—down to the banks of the San Juan where it cut through the Comb to facilitate our crossing of the only major river in our path. Once on the north bank, we would be off the reservation. I had an urgent message to deliver to our resupplier, but in the presence of Greg and Vaughn, I had to phrase it carefully. "When you meet us at the San Juan," I pleaded, "could you bring us some of that, um, you know what. . . ."

"What?"

"You know, the stuff that tastes so good after a long hot day of hiking."

"You mean beer?"

"You got it."

By 5:00 PM we had reached the blessed pothole full of water that I had discovered. Expecting to camp on the spot, I was surprised when Vaughn dropped his pack and immediately started hiking farther north. "I already looked," I said. My scout had included half a mile of domes beyond the providential pool. Vaughn didn't answer. Later he told me that he had hopes of stumbling onto a pothole I had missed, and relished the afternoon's stroll for its own sake.

I sat on the saddle, irritated once more. Didn't Vaughn trust me to scout? And so what if he found another pothole, a mile farther along?

From "my" reservoir, it was only a five-mile hike on the morrow to a reliable spring—the first spring anywhere in the forty-four miles we had covered on the Comb. The previous May I had day hiked in to that obscure bend of side-canyon, to make sure that the spring ran in even the driest weather. No matter what, we would be camping by that spring tomorrow night.

Vaughn returned after an hour. "It didn't rain here," he announced. "It's dry as shit. Not one drop. Not even a stain in the sand." It was my turn not to answer.

Later, over dinner, I would divine another reason for Vaughn's restless search for a farther campsite. We heard dogs barking from the homestead I had skirted, only half a mile to the southeast. Vaughn ventured the opinion that the dogs were reacting to our presence. I disagreed.

"I just don't like camping in someone's backyard," Vaughn insisted. "Some of these guys have pit bulls. That's what gives me the creeps."

Despite the persistence of our edgy relations, by the time I lay in my sleeping bag, staring through the tent netting at the familiar constellations, I felt a deep happiness. Tomorrow, when we reached the spring, we would begin our probe of a region that I had keenly looked forward to exploring for a year and a half—a fifteen-mile segment that promised to be geologically the most bizarre, but culturally the richest stretch in all the hundred-mile sweep of the Comb Ridge.

CHINLE

CHINLE WASH BEGINS AS AN INNOCUOUS trickle just north of the sleepy settlement of Ganado, Arizona, where John Lorenzo Hubbell established a trading post in 1878. (Today the old stone buildings are preserved as a National Historic Site.) For some thirty miles, the intermittent stream wanders north across the sands, drying up completely during rainless spells. At the town of Chinle, headquarters for Canyon de Chelly National Monument, the united flows of Canyon de Chelly and Canyon del Muerto (the sandstone fortress the Navajo had thought impregnable until Kit Carson laid waste to it in 1863–64) enter the wash from the east.

Onward into the north the Chinle meanders for another fifty miles, slipping under Highway 160 at the Navajo outpost of Tes Nez Iah, four miles west of Mexican Water. Here, the wash at last gets up the gumption to sculpt a canyon, albeit a modest, shallow one. For ten miles farther, the Chinle snakes across overgrazed badlands. Just north of Tes Nez Iah, it sneaks into Utah as obliviously as the three of us had on the morning of September 6.

Then suddenly, Chinle Wash collides with the Comb Ridge. The proud Cretaceous upthrust of 65 million years ago proved no match for gouging water. At latitude 37° 04' N., the stream carves a long U-bend of a channel clean through the Comb, emerging unfazed on its western edge. Any stream in its right mind, having pulled off such a tour de force, would trundle on into the northwest, slithering across the defenseless plain of Cane Valley to join the San Juan somewhere near Mexican Hat.

Not the Chinle. As if to show off its erosional prowess, two miles north of its escape from the escarpment, it makes an abrupt turn to the east to rip yet another gorge through the Comb Ridge. In the next seven miles as the crow flies, the stream breaches the Comb three more times, as if unable to make up its mind whether it prefers a channel east of the upthrust or west. At last, the Chinle succumbs to gravitational fatigue, surrendering its waters to the San Juan in a feeble, tamarisk- and willow-choked plod.

Chinle is Navajo for "place where water emerges from a canyon's mouth"—presumably in reference to that dramatic gate in the sandstone where the joined corridors of Canyon de Chelly and Canyon del Muerto burst onto the flats. But farther north, where the Chinle plays hide-and-seek with the Comb Ridge, some combination of water, wind, and Navajo sandstone creates a prodigal abundance of natural alcoves. The Anasazi knew a good thing when they saw it: shelter and running water.

Herbert Gregory, the pioneering geologist, reported in his 1916 treatise, *The Navajo Country*, that "during the rainy season and following showers" the Chinle "form[s] shallow lakes a mile or two in width." Perhaps that was true also in the thirteenth century, but it's been a long time now since anyone saw even a small pond in the canyon of the Chinle. Hiking in to the Comb to check out the vital spring in May 2004, I was shocked to find the Chinle completely dry. But several days before we launched our September traverse, Greg and I had flown over the Comb in a small plane piloted by our Bluff friend Gene Foushee, Greg to take pictures and I to look for water. I was heartened to see the blue gleam of flowing water in every bend of the Chinle where it performs its twisting surgery on the Comb.

Thus as we packed up camp on the morning of September 7, filling a mere six quart bottles per man from our pothole pool, we figured that from here to the San Juan, all our water problems ought to be solved. Where we couldn't find springs, we could drink the Chinle.

Some unknown Navajo artist had etched this proud horse into a cliff in an obscure corner of the reservation.

That day may have been the hottest so far on our trip. And for five miles, we found not an ounce of standing water. Either the violent storm of September 4 had somehow completely missed this stretch of Comb, or in less than three days evaporation had sucked the potholes dry. We trudged down ramps of orange slickrock and then a giant sand dune in which our feet sank ankle deep. Vaughn said, "Can you imagine if we had to hike *up* this mother?"

The one beguiling find of that half-day march was the finest single piece of Navajo rock art we would come across during our journey. On a buttress facing south, some Diné master of chisel or knife had engraved a horse in profile, striding from left to right. The interior surface of the animal had been rubbed gray, while the outlines of the horse were incised with some sharp tool. Unlike Anasazi zoomorphs, rigid and stylized, this proud stallion had been rendered with an exquisite naturalism that the painters of Lascaux might have envied. The very muscles of the animal in motion were precisely observed, the left foreleg raised in mid-canter. No engraved signature identified the artist.

We hit the banks of the Chinle shortly after noon. Our first glimpse of the stream delivered a mild shock. What had looked like a blue stream from a thousand feet above, in the backseat of Gene Foushee's airplane, turned out in reality to be an opaque chocolate flood—or perhaps the storm of September 4 had roiled the once-clear water into this gooey

Crossing Chinle Wash

muck. I took off my boots, seized a branch to use as a cane, and reconnoitered the stream without my pack. I sank in up to my thighs, my feet plunging into suckholes of quicksand invisible on the stream bottom. It was incredibly slippery going, but by concentrating on my balance, I made it across, and then back, where I shouldered my pack.

"Let's cross this, then have lunch in the first patch of shade we find," I suggested. Greg and Vaughn seemed to concur.

All three of us forded the Chinle without mishap. Any prospect of drinking the stream, however, had vanished: we knew that no amount of filtering or settling would render this liquid mud potable. On the far bank, Vaughn and I donned our Chaco sandals, rather than muddy our boots, while Greg (who had neglected to bring sandals) stumbled on barefoot. Immediately in front of us stood a tangled jungle, far taller than head-high, of tamarisks and willows.

Bashing our way through this thicket, cursing and breaking branches, we got separated. At last I broke free to the other side. I could hear Greg thrashing away behind me, so I sat down and waited till he appeared a minute or two later. We both sat and waited for Vaughn, but five minutes passed with no sign of him. I stood up and walked first down and then up the bank, thinking that he might have burst through the jungle out of sight of us and was waiting around a bend or two. At last I found his tracks, which without apparent hesitation climbed the arroyo bank to the shelf above.

I hurried back to Greg. "Goddamn Vaughn," I muttered, "he's always just taking off." Scrambling up the arroyo bank, I crested the river bench just in time to see Vaughn, several hundred yards away, about to disappear around a canyon corner. He was hiking fast. "Vaughn!" I shouted at the top of my lungs. It took four calls before he stopped and turned.

"What?" he shouted back.

Fuming, I closed the distance between us. When I was a few yards away, I said, "I thought we agreed to stop for lunch."

"We did?"

"Yeah, I brought it up right before we crossed the stream."

"I didn't hear you. I assumed we would meet at the spring."

Contemplating our trip during the months before we set out, I had concluded that there was little chance of our incurring a fatal or even a very serious accident on Comb Ridge. We were too experienced at hiking slickrock to do something stupid like fall off a cliff. But there were three things, I thought, that could sabotage or even terminate our trek. The first, and most likely, was a broken or badly sprained ankle, or a severely twisted knee. On the kind of terrain we were crossing daily, carrying loads that ranged from fifty-five to seventy-five pounds, such an injury was far from improbable. In that event, after the healthy pair had helped the cripple get out to a hospital, or at least to the refuge of a rocking chair, would they return to finish the hike as a twosome?

The second snafu would be to run out of water. In ninety-degree temperatures, with heavy packs, it's hard to go even a day without water, and the curve of thirsty deterioration is a steep one. Faced with too long a waterless stretch, we would be forced to bail off the Comb (probably to the east), hike to the nearest highway, and flag down a passing vehicle—or use our sat phone to call Jim Hook to our rescue.

The third potential screw-up, in my view, was if we got separated. From the day hikes we had already done on the non-reservation segments of the Comb, we had all learned how bewilderingly intricate the topography was, how one prong or col looked much like another. For me, the Comb was the hardest place in all the Southwest in which to remember the route to a given ruin or rock art panel. Even Vaughn had fooled himself on the Comb and momentarily "misplaced" sites he knew well.

If we got separated, how would we find each other and resume the traverse? I brought up this eventuality even before our trek began and suggested that every day we fix an agreed-upon rendezvous place, in case we lost track of one another. But Vaughn seemed to think such a precaution was silly, and Greg shrugged it off, too.

In 1964, on the first day of a two-man expedition to Mount Deborah in Alaska's Hayes Range, Don Jensen and I had started a forty-mile hike in to base camp on the West Fork Glacier. We had driven through the night to get to the stretch along the Denali Highway from which we would set out, and after a few hours of slogging across the spongy, swampy tundra with eighty-pound packs, we were exhausted.

Perhaps eight miles in, we stopped to rest on a dry log. I couldn't help falling asleep. The last thing I heard Don say was, "I'll just go ahead a little ways."

When I woke, I didn't know if thirty seconds or thirty minutes had elapsed. Don was nowhere in sight. I yelled his name, but got no answer. Deeply alarmed, I wrenched my pack onto my back and staggered forward, calling out every half minute. The flat tundra stretching to the horizon all looked the same. Don could have gone this way, or that, or that; or he could have stopped to wait for me, while I charged ahead on a different tack and passed him by.

In a kind of panic, I realized that our whole expedition could be jeopardized by this little glitch. If we failed to find each other, our only recourse would be to hike back all the way to the highway, hope to run into each other there, and start all over again the next day or the day after. Soon I was no longer sure whether Don was ahead of me or behind. Then, finally, I heard his distant answering call. At last he came in sight, barely visible beside a distant clump of alders. We joined up, both of us with sheepish grins on our faces. For the next forty-two days, we never lost sight of each other—except twice, when Don fell into a pair of huge crevasses, from the first of which it took half a day to extricate him.

Forty years later, I had come to recognize that on expeditions, I tended to be a congenital worrier, perhaps even an over-planner. But Vaughn's and Greg's blasé attitudes about getting separated were not going to convince me that such a turn would prove harmless. By September 7 my annoyance had been building through the previous two days. As we hiked the Comb, often side by side, we never designated one of us as the leader. But Vaughn, in particular, had a penchant for heading off on a certain vector without consulting Greg or me. If I suggested veering left to peer off the precipice and orient ourselves on the map, he would say, "Sure. I'll meet you up ahead." Rather than tempt fate, I would back down and follow his lead.

I had kept quiet about my annoyance, for fear of provoking an argument, but meanwhile the resentment had been building. Now it burst in a flood. "Goddamn it, Vaughn," I shouted, "the one thing that can fuck up our trip is if we get separated!"

Shocked at my anger, Vaughn answered aggressively: "That's ridiculous. The only danger is getting lost. And you can't get lost here. I thought we'd just meet at the spring."

"Greg doesn't even know where the spring is."

The quarrel persisted as we rejoined Greg and ate a tasteless lunch in the shade of the arroyo bank. "You just take off wherever you please," I complained. "I feel like yesterday I had no say at all in where we got to go."

"I do sort of take off. But we were never out of sight of each other."

"You would have been just now if I hadn't come after you."

"Geez, nobody's gonna get lost here."

"Christ, Vaughn! Of course we're not going to get lost. Separated. Don't you know the difference?"

"I could find somebody by his tracks."

I let out an exasperated sigh. "What do you gain by doing all this?"

Greg had had enough. "Stop it!" he barked. "It's not even an issue!"

We finished our lunch in a pained silence. Underneath my self-righteous anger, I felt shame and sorrow. In eight years of friendship, I had never before lost my temper like this at Vaughn. Thanks in large part to his equanimity and distaste for conflict, we had never had a serious argument.

Yet Vaughn's headlong flights here on the Comb puzzled me. Hiking on Cedar Mesa, we had never felt this kind of tension. There, if Vaughn or I had a hunch about which direction to head next, one of us would say, "How about following this ledge around the next corner?" Even on Edgeøya, the uninhabited island in the Svalbard archipelago, beset with fogs and whiteouts, we had gone out of our way to stick together, in no small part because of the ever-present menace of polar bears.

Weeks later, Vaughn would clarify his position on that hot September day. "I'm so used to keeping track of people guiding," he told me, "and hiking with people like Fred Blackburn, who's always taking off, that I guess I don't worry so much. I grew up hunting with people who went off their different ways, but we always got back together."

We reached the spring at 2:00 PM. As I had seen the previous May, the generous seep pouring out of its bedrock seam, tucked in a corner of side-canyon under arching walls, made for a cozy, blissful campsite. Tall trees gave us shade against the withering heat. The water looked so pure that we might have been tempted to drink it unfiltered, but there were animal tracks around the spring, so we played it safe.

We relaxed through the early afternoon, as the slickrock inferno gradually cooled. Vaughn and Greg were having foot problems. After the first day, when I had taped the hot spots on the balls of my feet, I had been lucky enough to avoid all blister problems. Now Vaughn was developing his own hot spots, while Greg's boots, a bit too narrow in the front, were starting to pinch and bruise his toes.

In mid-afternoon, I volunteered to reconnoiter ahead, looking for potholes, now that we knew the Chinle was undrinkable. (After the trip, a Navajo friend of Vaughn's from Bluff, who had lived much of his life on a plateau just east of the Chinle, told him that he had never in any season found the stream clear enough to drink.) Making a two-hour loop, I found only one usable tank, but it was a deep one full of clear rainwater, and that discovery was worth the trip. As I stumbled wearily back into camp, Greg saw my florid face and said, "You look fried."

The hard feelings of midday had ebbed. After dinner we sat drinking tea around the spring. We felt a delicious sense of reprieve, for we had agreed to leave our camp in place the next day, spending the hours instead on loop hikes to explore the nearby cliffs for Anasazi sites. For the first time on the trip, we could enjoy a whole day without humping our heavy loads.

As dusk descended on us, Greg and Vaughn pitched their tents and laid out their sleeping bags. "You gonna read to us in bed again?" Vaughn asked.

In general, on our Comb traverse we had gone as light and frugal on gear as we could. But Vaughn and Greg were carrying heavy cameras and lenses, while I had brought along not even a point-and-shoot. That economy allowed me to rationalize the two luxuries I had indulged myself in. One was a Crazy Creek chair—the hinge of sheathed Ensolite that made a handy, portable seat. For a week now, Vaughn and Greg had mercilessly teased me about this extravagance, and I had teased back: "You know," I would say as I scribbled notes in my journal, "it's important for the writer to be comfortable while he's getting down all the details you guys will promptly forget." I pleaded with them to occupy the chair when I wasn't using it, but—true to their spartan self-denial—not once on the long trek did either of them succumb.

My other luxury was a single book, to be swapped for another at each resupply. Two nights earlier, at our serene camp by the five giant potholes, I had offered to read aloud by headlamp, propped in my chair, while Vaughn and Greg lay snug in their sleeping bags. "This is great," Vaughn had said halfway through my recital. "It's like having an audio book."

The volume I was reading was *Traders to the Navajos*, an as-told-to memoir published by Frances Gillmor in 1934. Both Vaughn and I had read the book before, but many years ago. *Traders* was the ideal work to be reading now, for it recounted the extraordinary adventures of John and Louisa Wetherill, who in 1906 had outfaced Navajo threats to build a trading post first at Oljato, and then, four years later, at Kayenta—the first trading post in the most remote part of the Navajo Reservation, which happened to be the country just west of the Comb Ridge. During those decades at the beginning of the twentieth century, John Wetherill had become the premier guide and explorer in the Four Corners region, spearheading (among other exploits) the Anglo discovery of Rainbow Bridge in 1909.

For the most part, *Traders* is a lyrical, even romantic account of the frontier life. But it contains one sublime set piece of tragicomedy—a passage both Vaughn and I had long forgotten. It has to do with a conflict between a Navajo named Hosteen Chee and a half-Navajo, half-Paiute named Natani. In this imbroglio, Louisa Wetherill—known to the natives as Asthon Sosi, the "Slim Woman"—tried to act as peacemaker.

It happened to be that night that I read those pages out loud. For some reason (relief from our noontime quarrel must have played a part), the passage reduced all three of us to hysterics. Because of its impact on us, the excerpt may be worth quoting at some length.

Hosteen Chee has come to Asthon Sosi with a complaint. "'Natani has been riding my horses again,' he said. 'He has ridden one of them to death.'" The Slim Woman urges the Navajo to report his gripe to the tribal policeman, but Hosteen Chee demurs.

At last Hosteen Chee makes a suggestion:

"Don't you think I ought to shoot him?" he said. "He has been riding my horses. He has done other things that all the People know about. I think I ought to shoot him."
Asthon Sosi protested emphatically.
"No! You must not shoot Natani."
"I think I ought to."
"You must not shoot Natani."
"I have already shot Natani," announced Hosteen Chee.
"You have shot him! Is he dead?"
"I don't know. It was dark in his hogan. I shot him three times until he cried out, 'Do not shoot again, brother, for you have hit me.' But I don't know where I hit him."

Before I was halfway through this dialogue, I was gasping and crying with laughter. I couldn't finish "I have already shot Natani" without my voice screeching into a wail. Nearby, Vaughn and Greg were howling, too. In bits and pieces, I read and reread the passage several times over, like a joke so good you have to retell it immediately upon finishing. We must have been convulsed for twenty minutes. We would catch our breaths, and I would try to read on, only to have one of us start giggling, unleashing general hysterics all over again.

Laughter so insane was the best possible cure for our sometime-doldrums. And throughout the rest of the trip, apropos of nothing, even while we were hiking along, Greg would suddenly adopt a solemn voice and, mimicking some Grade-B-western Indian, blurt out, "I think I ought to shoot him." Thus Hosteen Chee and Natani became the mascots of our voyage.

You could hardly call September 8 a rest day, but it felt like one. Vaughn and I set out, each on his own loop, for eight-hour excursions among the canyon bends and alcoves, while Greg stayed closer to camp, composing camera portraits of this supremely photogenic stretch of Comb Ridge. I chose to head south, up the Chinle, while Vaughn set off downstream on an entirely different route.

One might well ask why, if I had been so bent out of shape the day before at the prospect of our getting separated after the thrash through the tamarisks, I was willing now for all three of us to spend the day apart, each fulfilling the whims of his solo jaunt. It was the fixed camp that made all the difference. There was indeed no danger of our getting lost on the Comb. The camp beside the spring would be our rendezvous point at the end of day.

Had I been able to get my comrades to agree to such a prearranged rendezvous spot for each day of backpacking, I doubt that Vaughn and I would have ever locked horns. We might then have wandered out of sight and hearing of each other with minimal harm or nuisance. Of course, it would have been harder to designate a rendezvous place somewhere miles ahead, at a location we had yet to find, than at the temporary base camp beside the spring where our tents were already pitched. But a simple pledge—"If we get separated, we'll meet tonight on the north side of Moses Rock" (Moses Rock being a soaring tower you could see from miles around)—would have resolved my qualms. Yet stubborn to the core, all three of us, we could not forge such a protocol.

After a week of close company, it felt great to hike alone. For several miles, I followed the east bank of the Chinle upstream. Sometimes this afforded easy walking on flat benches, but side-arroyos occasionally dissected the terrain into nasty mini-chasms of petrified mud. Crossing some of these amounted to perilous scrambling on the verge of the technical: with a sixty-pound pack, I thought, these unstable fins and cliffs of hard-packed dirt would have been impossible to climb.

All along the way, I kept finding signs of the Anasazi: a couple of single-room masoned structures on ledges fifty to eighty feet above the valley floor, a scattering of white and dark-red lithics here, a fan of red-on-orange potsherds there. Rounding a bend I spotted three burros on the shelf below, browsing among the grasses beside the Chinle. Their coats were black and white, with white ovals around their eyes against otherwise black heads, making them look as though they were wearing goggles. A moment later, three other burros came out of the willows to join them. These beasts, for sure, were wild, for all over the West once-tame burros had gone feral, and it was too much work for their former owners to catch them. I spotted the burros before they saw me. When they did, all six froze, staring up at the two-legged intruder. A couple of them snorted in fear or warning, their strange rasping honks echoing loud off the canyon wall behind me, but they did not bolt.

All too soon, it was getting close to turn-around time. From a high perch, I stared as far as I could up the Chinle, where it meandered through the canyon it had carved before clashing with the Comb Ridge. I promised myself another hike in another year, perhaps a descent of the whole hundred miles of the ruin-rich Chinle.

Above me and to the left gaped a deep, round alcove facing northwest. "Basketmaker, I'll bet," I said out loud.

Cliff dwellings such as the handsome one we had found on the first day on the Comb are almost exclusively the work of Anasazi during the last two centuries before their 1300 abandonment of the Four Corners region. Besides serving an evident defensive function, those masoned villages tend to face south. The overhanging wall that forms the alcove thus casts shade on the dwellings in summer, when the sun is high, but gathers the heat of the low sun in winter. This seems an ideal solution to the challenge of living in the desert Southwest, but a thousand years and more before the cliff dwellers, the Anasazi chose a very different sort of alcove in which to live and bury their dead. These gaping mouths in the cliffs tend to be low ceilinged, dark, and usually north facing. To our modern sensibility, alcoves like these seem utterly gloomy places to live, and the choice of such sites remains a phenomenon poorly explained by archaeologists. Over the years, Vaughn and I—and by now, Greg—had learned to spot the signature of a Basketmaker cave from a distance.

In 1927 the great archaeologist Alfred V. Kidder called together all the leading Southwestern scholars for a conference at the site he was in the process of excavating, Pecos Pueblo in northern New Mexico. The Pecos Conference has been held virtually every August since, though at many different places besides Pecos. At that first gathering, the savants worked out the taxonomy of Anasazi phases that is still in wide use across the Southwest. The earliest sites were dubbed Basketmaker—a term already in use, referring to a people who made beautiful baskets out of yucca, willow, and dogbane (some so tightly woven they could hold water) but had no pottery.

The Pecos archaeologists postulated two phases of Basketmaker culture, which they called Basketmaker II and III. The scholars' judgment was that those oldest sites already bespoke such sophistication in the material culture that there must have been an earlier, more primitive phase out of which Basketmaker II developed. But the hypothetical Basketmaker I phase has never been discovered. Instead, hunter-gatherers, during the era archaeologists call the Archaic, roaming the Southwest as early as 6500 BC, blend seamlessly into the first semisedentary denizens of Basketmaker II.

After Basketmaker III, the Pecos archaeologists broke prehistory into four further phases, dubbed Pueblo I, II, III, and IV. Pueblo IV stretched from the abandonment of the Four Corners up into the sixteenth century and first contact with the Spanish. In 1927 the technique of tree-ring dating had yet to be discovered. The scholars could affix no absolute dates to their phases, only a relative chronology based on stratigraphy—the obvious yet powerful principle that in general, stuff found lower in the soil is older than stuff found on top of it.

Thanks to tree rings, we can now assign a date around AD 750 for the transition from Basketmaker III to Pueblo I. It was originally thought that the Basketmakers were a separate people, dislodged and perhaps exterminated by the invading Pueblo culture. In the 1940s, however, archaeologists proved that the two were one—all

Anasazi, who also stretch back into the Archaic, though how far we may never know.

Now I scrambled up toward the small cavity in the cliff facing northwest. It was brutal going—steep slabby plates of sandstone that tended to crack and slide underfoot, and then a dense stand of scrub oak that choked the whole mouth of the cave, through which I slithered, scraping bloody scratches on my arms and legs. I almost gave up, but a peek through binoculars at the dim back wall hinted at rock art.

Yes, it was indeed a gloomy place. Gazing out from its deepest recesses, I realized that the cave would receive no sunlight all year long. What was going on with these troglodytes? Even the shrewdest archaeologists have never adequately explained the Basketmaker preference for cramped, cold, north-facing alcoves.

But what a find! In the fine dirt on the floor, I came across a number of cists, slab-lined pentagons that probably served as storage chambers.

The glory of the site, however, was its rock art. It has taken several centuries of western art criticism to dispel the notion of history as progress. In European churches Romanesque frescoes are no longer viewed as crude, angular cartoons that pave the way for the refined splendor of the Gothic. Nowhere is the fallacy that art gets better through the ages more striking than in the Southwest. If anything, Basketmaker pictographs and petroglyphs tend to outclass the later Pueblo panels. On a San Juan River float trip in 1994, I had been tickled to see Polly Schaafsma, the leading expert on Southwestern rock art, point to some last-gasp Pueblo III petroglyphs before our eyes and dismiss them as "mere doodling."

The back wall of the cave was covered with a swath of painted figures. Seven bright red handprints on the left balanced six faint yellow ones on the right. A zigzag orange-red "snake" crawled toward nowhere. The composition was anchored by three "crescent-headed anthropomorphs," as the experts dryly characterize these magisterial figures. Face on, arms and legs spread wide, these humanoids have broad shoulders that taper through the torso into narrow waists. Only one of the three anthropomorphs had an actual head, rendered simply as an oval blob of white paint; but all three were crowned by "crescents," long arcing curves that looked something like boomerangs. Some scholars think the crescents stand for trance states undergone by shamans; others see them as actual headdresses, perhaps the very *tablitas* found, though rarely, in excavations.

The masterpiece of the panel was its central figure, a finely drawn anthropomorph in dark red paint, rendered as a Picasso-like, stylized form that seemed about to slip into the abstract. The arms and legs simply ended in nothing, handless and footless. Down the chest dangled a fourteen-cornered zigzag—snake (or lightning strike?) as pendant. The head, detached from the body, was reduced to a double chevron, two crescents, without a hint of eyes, nose, or mouth.

What was it all about? I had no idea—but that didn't keep me from staring for long minutes as, for the first time ruing my failure to bring a camera, I sketched the paintings into my journal.

Nor was this all. The bedrock boulders lying on the floor of the cave were covered with petroglyphs: a wiggly anthropomorph dangling a three-fanged penis longer than his legs, a whirling pinwheel like a comet, an antlered humanoid with split-level arms. Most beguiling of all was a track of four bear-paw prints in a row, each pecked on a separate boulder, as if the bear had moved through the site in graceful bounds from stone to stone.

At last I headed back toward camp, taking the high road on top of the Comb rather than retrace my steps along the Chinle bench and have to recross the nasty side-arroyos. All over the cliff top, there were a lot of potholes, but every one had dried up.

Back in camp, I swapped discoveries with Vaughn, who had just arrived, red faced and tired. His first words to Greg were, "It was more than a two-quart day out there." On an equally demanding loop of his own, downstream to the north, he too had found marvels of rock art, including one crowded frieze of Basketmaker petroglyphs, perhaps a hundred different figures, twenty-five feet up a vertical cliff, where the ground on which the artists had once stood had subsided and eroded over the eons to strand the panel in thin air.

We agreed this had been our best day yet on the Comb. But it was only the beginning of a five-day string of dazzling finds, a spell so magical and intense that we would reach the south bank of the San Juan River with our minds blown and our spirits steeped in the enigmatic beauty the Anasazi had left behind as legacy of their presence.

It was along this stretch that we came across the single most astounding site we would find on the Comb, a ruin that we would spend parts of two days exploring. On a ledge a hundred feet above the Chinle, all along a sharp inward bend of the stream, beneath a severely over-hanging wall that soars 200 feet to the cliff top, the Anasazi had built a village facing southwest, comprising at least seventy to seventy-five rooms. In its defensive grandeur, the place is solid Pueblo III in date. It is, in fact, the largest cliff dwelling in Utah.

Anglo-American explorers or military officers in the 1850s may have been the first non-Native Americans to discover the ruin, but the first to report it was a government surveyor and photographer who found the site in the 1870s. It was he who gave the ruin the name by which it has been informally known ever since.

At such an early date, archaeology in the United States was hardly distinguishable from pothunting and arrowhead collecting. Heading up the Chinle from its mouth on the San Juan, the explorer's party un-abashedly "picked up many arrows, knives, and other stone implements, with the ever-present pottery." The idea was to gather everything in sight, making little or no record of its provenience, or context on the ground, haul it back to some museum or university, and only then be-gin to study what the artifacts might signify. Digging in the midden, or rubbish heap, below the ruin, the team unearthed "seven large earthen pots of rough indented ware." These pots were probably *ollas*—massive water jugs. At least the team had the good sense not to ruin them in the process of claiming them for science. As the explorer wrote in his report, "They were too fragile to admit of transportation upon pack-animals, so we put them carefully by for future investigators."

Nonetheless, in the bland positivism of the explorer's prose, there lurks the sense of unlimited riches to be had for the taking: "A careful search through the very thick deposits of *débris* would undoubtedly reveal many treasures, and we felt many regrets that we could not consistently devote a number of days to the pleasant un-dertaking." Sixty-five years later, the memory of that regret comes across undimmed in the explorer's autobiography. Of that prodigal site on the Chinle, he writes,

> *Although it had been abandoned centuries before, the accumulated débris was rich in relics. Glazed pottery (mostly fragments), hollowed stone grinding basins, ax heads, arrow tips, and spear points abounded. Only our need to travel light kept us from departing with an immense haul.*

Nearly half a century would elapse between the explorer's pioneering reconnaissance of this matchless cliff dwelling and the first professional archaeologist's study of it. The latter scholar's team spent two weeks excavating the ancient village. As he wryly noted in his own report, during that five-decade interim, "the ruin seems to have escaped attention, except by pothunters, who have broken a number of holes through the bases of walls for the easier disposal of rubbish. Seven large ollas that [the 1870s surveyor] speaks of having found and left in the site had, of course, disappeared."

The 1920s archaeologist's methods of digging and reporting were models for the day. But by the standards of our own age, the former seems unnecessarily rapacious, the latter all too cursory. The excavators found their own lodes of treasure, including a subterranean burial chamber containing the skeleton of a man wrapped in an elaborate "fur- and feather-string blanket." Beside the man lay his grave goods: a broken bow and arrow, three baskets, and four pieces of pottery. Perhaps the most remarkable find made by the 1920s team was a small "cache-pot" full of objects that must have had a special meaning to the Anasazi, including one of the most remarkable artifacts ever found in the Southwest: in the words of the archaeologist, a "mosaic incrusted flaked knife blade."

A good color drawing of this masterwork would later serve as the frontispiece to the archaeologist's report. Yet how much comfort can today's reader take in the knowledge that the mosaic-encrusted blade lies now in some storage drawer in the museum of an eastern university, where no one bothers for years at a time to look at it, much less puzzle out its meaning?

For all the team's two weeks of digging in the site, precious little insight emerged from their toil. The report carefully describes the ruin and the artifacts, but makes no stab at interpretation. The very anomalies of the place, which would strike our own eyes so forcefully in 2004, are duly noted but left for later scholars to explain.

In the eight decades since the 1920s team worked in the cliff dwelling, as far as I know, no further serious archaeology has been undertaken there. The largest cliff dwelling in Utah has yet even to be dated by tree-ring cores. Meanwhile, later pothunters have wreaked their own havoc in the site.

Yet herein lies the cardinal anomaly of all. Both the 1870s surveyor and the 1920s archaeologist remarked on how fragile the ruin looked. To our eyes, too, it looked incredibly fragile—a hard push, one suspected, could easily collapse a two-story wall that had stood for more than seven centuries. Yet the 1920s scholar compared his own photograph of one section of the ruin with the exact same picture taken by the surveyor in the 1870s. As the former wrote in his report, "During the fifty-year period there appears to have been no perceptible change. Loose rocks at the tops of the walls and in fallen walls lie in the same positions in both photographs. It seems then that the natural decay of time is an almost negligible factor in the destruction of ruins situated such as this one."

Later we would compare our own photographs to the one taken by the 1920s savant. A few walls had collapsed during the eighty years between his visit and ours, but the paradox was inescapable.

In a deep dry alcove beneath a tall cliff on a bend of Chinle Wash lies this two-story free-standing building.

The seemingly fragile cliff dwelling had a phenomenal staying power. The Anasazi had built it to last, and they had known what they were doing.

The decorum that Greg and I observed as we tiptoed through this incomparable lost village was in fact the only permissible regimen for non-professionals visiting any backcountry ruin in the first decade of the twenty-first century. (Vaughn, who had visited the site two decades before, went off on further excursions of his own while we explored the ruin.) Our impact had to be lighter than light: ideally, our passing would make no impact at all. To that end, we crossed the midden only on the faint trail previous passersby had worn in a diagonal ascent to the cliff dwelling itself. We never sat or stepped on a room wall: we did not, indeed, even touch the walls of the still-standing rooms. If we picked up a sherd of Tusayan polychrome, we put it back exactly where we had found it. For the most part, we simply walked as gingerly as we could across the bedrock floor on which the ruin had been built, staring, commenting, photographing, and sketching.

In the face of such a prehistoric prodigy, mere description fails. Suffice it to note some of the place's wonders: a free-standing wall with windows, three stories tall (one of very few unrestored walls that tall anywhere in the Southwest); a perfectly preserved, spacious two-story dwelling, with twin windows on the upper floor, a T-shaped doorway leading into the lower; rooms that incorporated boulders strewn on the ledge in an architecture so cunning, Le Corbusier himself might have envied it; chipped hand-and-toe trails leading from one level to the next; "coat pegs," or sticks mortared into the interior walls of rooms, perhaps to hang things from; several big, round subterranean kivas, their inner walls still plastered; beam sockets bored into the cliff itself, so far off the ledge that they must have anchored roofs of three-story structures that had since vanished.

All across the cliff face at the back of the alcove sprawled a gallery of pictographs: just above the three-story wall, a giant white "shield" serrated with vertical lines; humanoids with rings or hairbobs dangling from their ears; round-bellied, headless anthropomorphs striding comically to the left; spirals, snakes, designs that looked almost like Mayan hieroglyphs. At some point I stopped sketching and simply catalogued the different hues of paint. "White," I wrote in my journal, "copper brown, creamy white, green, maroon, reddish-orange, brown (mud), yellow, black (charcoal), dark reddish-brown

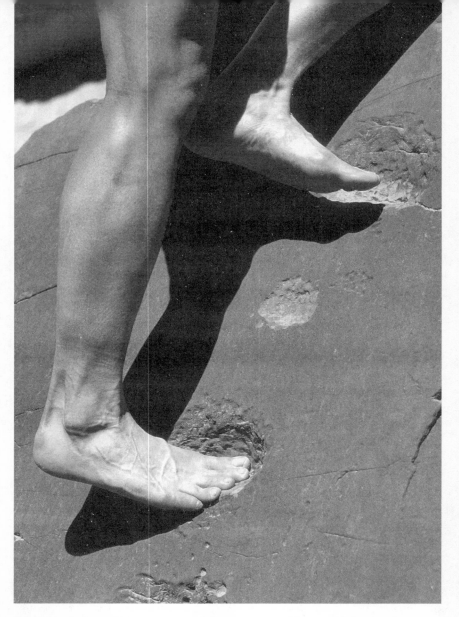

Hand and toe trails to get up and down canyon sides were laboriously chipped into cliffs with stone tools.

(rust)"—each color requiring a different mineral or plant from which to extract the precious paint.

    We found a few graffiti. In what looked to me like an early twentieth-century hand, some scribe had recorded the evening's dinner:

MINUE [MENU]
BISCUIT
TOMATOO SPAGHETTI
COFFEE.

Far more infuriating was the crescent symbol of the Boy Scouts, drawn in yellow crayon, with the motto, "BSA TROOP 35." A few old charcoal signatures had almost faded away. The names of those early cowboys—Navajo or Anglo?—meant nothing to us. And we found the 1920s archaeologist's record of his site number, neatly lettered in white paint—a graffito just as surely as the Boy Scout emblem, but the practice of the day.

As I stood looking at pictographs, I heard a sudden sharp report. Every climber knows in his guts the sound of falling rocks, so I instinctively ducked and threw my left arm over my head. Several huge stones flew into view, and then thudded into the midden, a good forty feet beyond the outermost dwelling—thereby demonstrating the overhang's protective function, though shelter from rain and snow must have been more important to the Anasazi than relief from the occasional falling rock.

It was only after hours of prowling through the long ruin that I fully appreciated its most salient feature. The ledge on which this lordly village had been erected was actually not a very good place for building. In consequence, the right-hand or eastern half of the ruin had been constructed smack on top of a talus pile. The cleverness with which the rooms had been fitted among and on top of boulders was admirable, but all that debris must still have been a nuisance to the inhabitants.

It was in the left-hand or western end of the site, where its best-preserved structures were thronged, that an even more extreme building technique had been exacted from the ancients. There, the natural ledge below the overhang was not even close to horizontal: instead, it pitched downward at angles ranging from twenty to forty-five degrees. To erect the roomblocks here (including the still-standing three-story wall), the Anasazi had had to haul tons of fill—dirt and small stones—and somehow mason it in place on the tilting slab, so that the dwelling above it might have a level floor. Yet some of the finest and largest rooms had been engineered thus, on the western edge of the village.

East of the great talus pile, a pair of upper-level "suburbs," each occupying its own mini-alcove, complemented the main ruin. Greg found a hand-and-toe trail up to the nearest one, requiring a climb only about 5.1 in difficulty. He and I prowled through this Anasazi attic. The back wall of the cliff had been painted with nine large white oval disks or "shields," with a line of white dots connecting them. Here, too, the dwellings had been built on steep slabs, with fill making a level floor. Not one dwelling had a window facing out. As I wrote in my journal, "Crazy—marginal. A last-ditch refuge?"

The other upper-story suburb, even Greg could find no way to reach. Perhaps the Anasazi had leaned a series of log ladders against the seventy-degree cliff that guarded the high dwellings. (Elsewhere in the Southwest, we had found such ladders, a few still in place.)

No matter how magnificent this cliff dwelling seemed to us, there was no escaping the conclusion that the primary motive that had shaped the village was defense. But whom were the ancients afraid of, and why?

From the 1870s on, Anglos who discovered and marveled over the cliff dwellings came to the same seemingly obvious conclusion: these stone-and-mud towns tucked into caves in the cliffs were fortresses against attackers. And the fact that the cliff dwellings were all abandoned meant that at some point in the past the invaders had won.

Beginning with Coronado's 1540–1542 *entrada*, the Spaniards who explored and then conquered Nuevo México made frequent observation of the fact that, year after year, the Puebloans in their inward-looking villages were subjected to constant raids from the nomadic Indians who surrounded them on all sides: Navajos, Apaches, Utes, and Comanches. Surely the same thing had happened to the Puebloans' ancestors, the Anasazi who had abandoned the cliff dwellings.

For most of a century, then, the going theory was that nomadic peoples—Utes, Navajos, and Apaches were the leading candidates—had driven the Anasazi out of their Four Corners heartland. It was only as the study of numerous archaeological sites left by the nomads stubbornly refused to yield a date anywhere close to 1300 that that theory was cast into doubt. Today, virtually no scholars believe the Athapaskans (Apaches and Navajos) contributed to the abandonment. A few experts still think that Numic peoples (probably Utes and Shoshone) could have drifted in from Nevada's Great Basin as early as the twelfth century and put pressure on the Anasazi, but those archaeologists are distinctly in the minority.

Meanwhile, careful examination of ruins and artifacts was amassing abundant evidence of an environmental crisis gripping the Colorado Plateau in the thirteenth century. Tree rings revealed a severe drought between 1276 and 1299. The fact that Anasazi arrowheads get steadily smaller through the centuries suggested that the people may have hunted the big game to near-extinction. As early as 1925, a prescient scholar named Kirk Bryan had found evidence of a catastrophic phenomenon he called arroyo cutting. We now believe that arroyo cutting can be caused by some mysterious geological trigger or by human impact, such as the overgrazing by Anglo and Navajo cattle and sheep in the 1890s that unleashed a scourge of arroyo cutting all over the Four Corners region. In either case, within a matter of only a few years, the water table drastically plummets as streams carve arroyos (the very same cliff-like mud banks I had clambered across on my hike up the Chinle on September 8), leaving the once-fertile fields on the benches above completely arid. And Bryan and others documented a major episode of arroyo cutting in the second half of the thirteenth century. Finally, other scholars began to speculate that the insatiable demand for wood—both for roof beams and for fires to cook food and to heat dwellings—had caused the Anasazi to deforest their homeland.

Today, nearly all the experts believe that the principal cause of the abandonment was that environmental crisis. Unable to hang on in the Four Corners, the Anasazi emigrated en masse to the south and east, amalgamating with Puebloans already in place along the Rio Grande and the Little Colorado River, as well as on the Hopi mesas. Yet the puzzle is not so neatly solved. If the 1276–99 drought was the final straw, why could the Anasazi not have taken refuge on the banks of the Colorado or the San Juan Rivers, reliably fed every year by snows in the mountains of their headwaters in Colorado and Wyoming? What was the advantage of the Rio Grande over the Colorado? How could the Anasazi continue to grow corn on the Hopi mesas, and not on Cedar Mesa?

In the 1990s a mega-hypothesis, nicknamed the "push-pull" theory, came into vogue. Yes, the environmental crisis had been the push that drove the Anasazi out of the Four Corners, but such a complete and irreversible migration required also a pull—something going on to the south and east that the Anasazi up north and west got wind of and found too appealing to resist. At the time I wrote *In Search of the Old Ones* (published in 1996), many experts were touting the invention of the Kachina Phenomenon as the pull, and I wrote that theory into my book. The Kachina Phenomenon (or Cult, as it was called before the PC revisionists cleaned up our language) is a religion based on some four hundred semi-supernatural beings who intercede between the gods and the people, ensuring rain, fertility, and health. The kachinas are impersonated by masked dancers in elaborate ceremonies held in plazas and kivas. This new religion, we are fairly sure, sprang up first either near the Little Colorado or along the Rio Grande.

The Kachina Phenomenon serves to integrate large communities across all kinds of boundaries of clan and moiety and kinship groups. And integrating is a good thing, especially if you are besieged by nomadic raiders. The phenomenon has proved remarkably durable, for—despite the ruthless imposition of the Catholic faith by the Spaniards from 1598 on as well as the tireless conversion efforts of Anglo evangelicals in the twentieth century—kachinas still anchor Puebloan religion. But a decade after the theory was advanced, the Kachina Phenomenon as the abandonment pull is no longer in vogue. The main problem is that, despite assiduous research, no one has yet found clear evidence (in the form of icons representing kachina masks on rock art panels, pottery, or kiva murals) from before 1325. If the phenomenon first took hold a quarter century after the abandonment, it could hardly have been the great "pull."

This is not to dismiss the idea of a pull altogether. Pueblo ethnographers have recorded many an old story of the people long ago receiving injunctions from their gods to migrate. Movement en masse, in response not only to drought and famine, but to spiritual mandates received by visionary chiefs and shamans, is built into the very fabric of Puebloan life. Yet just what injunction at the end of the thirteenth century could have pulled the Anasazi out of their Four Corners heartland remains an unsolved question.

Back to the cliff dwellings. Once tree-ring dates had anchored the chronology beyond the shadow of a doubt, it became clear that all across the Four Corners, sometime in the twelfth century and throughout the thirteenth, the Anasazi turned their backs on a way of living that was centuries old—that of largely undefended, open-air pueblos built on mesa tops and river benches—and moved into alcoves in the cliffs, where they walled themselves up in hyper-defensive villages. In retrospect, it seems shocking that it took so long for archaeologists to accept what they themselves call the most parsimonious explanation for this shift—the one that most easily fits all the data. But beginning with the Spanish conquistadors and friars in the sixteenth century, who saw the house-building Puebloans as a more advanced form of civilization than that of the "savage" no-mads who roamed from place to place, a powerful but unexamined predilection to see Pueblo people (and their ancestors) as peaceful Indians held sway.

It was, we must now admit, the Anasazi themselves who were the enemy. In the face of famine and drought, a good supply of stored corn means the difference between life and death. During the hard times of the thirteenth century, the Anasazi of one village began to raid and kill their neighbors. The best defense against such attacks was an impregnable cliff dwelling.

To Vaughn, Greg, and me, this explanation always seemed obvi-ous. On Cedar Mesa and elsewhere, the very hardest ruins for us to climb to had almost always been granaries. Better to give up one's home than one's corn. Yet it took hard-core archaeology—epitomized by the brilliant study undertaken around Marsh Pass in Arizona by husband-and-wife team Winifred Creamer and Jonathan Haas, pub-lished in 1993 as *Stress and Warfare among the Kayenta Anasazi of the Thirteenth Century*—to clinch the case. There are still skeptics. "Where are all the dead bodies?" they protest. "We're just starting to find them," Creamer and Haas would answer. What is more, you don't necessarily have to kill your enemy to steal his corn. In the late thirteenth century, raiding was more important even than war.

Yet in the end, no strategy for dealing with the crisis worked. One day perhaps in the 1270s or 1280s, the last inhabitants of the proudest cliff dwelling on Chinle Wash gave up the struggle. They packed up a modicum of essential belongings and started marching south and east. No doubt they planned to come back, for they left behind their most treasured belongings, such as that mosaic-encrusted flaked knife blade, safely tucked away in pots hidden among the roomblocks.

But they never did come back. Instead, they left their village to crumble slowly over the centuries. Yet thanks to the overhang that guarded it, the cliff dwelling kept its essential shape and integrity, trans-muting into the handsome ruin that Greg and I would wander through and wonder at more than seven hundred years later.

⸺⧓⸺

Greg and I slept each night in our spiffy one-man North Face Mountain Marathon tents, which weighed a mere two pounds apiece. Vaughn preferred a reinforced bivouac sack that, with a curved pole to hold the netting aloft above his face, made for an even snugger enclosure. On our second night camped by the spring, he had been awakened by a kangaroo rat or a deer mouse that was scampering across his body and burrowing among our pots. Vaughn shooed it away, but as we packed up in the morning, he cursed, "That little bastard."

"What's the matter?" I asked.

"Critter chewed holes in my suck tube." Vaughn held up the mu-tilated piece of plastic tubing that fed water from the bladder inside his pack to his mouth. "It's unfixable."

As we hoisted our packs, I joked, "The moral of the story is, don't camp at a spring."

"The moral of the story," Vaughn rejoined, "is don't camp two nights in the same place."

He was right. All three of us had witnessed the process by which varmints in the wilderness first discover the presence of humans with all their exotic goodies, and then grow bold enough to turn into scav-engers and pilferers. Two or three days was the usual familiarization span. I thought of Canada jays in the Colorado mountains in winter— "camp robbers," as they are affectionately dubbed. Invisible through the first day, they make their timid appearance on the second, hop-ping on the outskirts of camp. By the third or fourth day, they are as blasé and obnoxious as the pigeons in St. Mark's Square in Venice.

We recrossed the slimy Chinle near camp and found a decent track through the tamarisk jungle that I had scouted the day before. Soon we had regained the bench on the west bank of the stream.

We had been uncertain how to follow the Comb through the next several miles, cut into pieces as it was by the meandering but indomita-ble Chinle. Vaughn's solo loop downstream on September 8 had made it clear that we could not possibly carry backpacks along the streambed itself. Between quicksand, tamarisks and willows and poison ivy, and

Previous, below, and opposite pages: *On a bend of the Chinle Wash on the Navajo reservation lies one of the largest Anasazi ruins in Utah, replete with a lofty tower wall.*

Moqui steps lead into this boulder-top structure above Chinle Wash.

Looking north along the Comb from beyond midway, the end in sight

A pocket of moisture in a bay of the Comb brought these wildflowers to bloom amid an otherwise arid sandscape.

Cactus points and ancient point poking out of a dune

David (left) and Vaughn on the Comb, beneath untraversable pinnacles on the crest

Previous page caption: *A weird halo cloud caps the setting sun beside the sacred Navajo peak of Agathla.*

A village tucked into an inaccessible cliff ledge, above Chinle Wash

The sun, an upside-down man (perhaps signifying death?), a headless figure, ritualistic objects, and birds ascending—this petroglyph panel tells a tale, but its meaning is long lost.

Ridge upon ridge upon ridge. Looking north over ballooning slickrock humps on Comb Ridge

Fins of sandstone radiate out from the Comb near its origin near Kayenta, Arizona.

On the crest of the Comb we got water from this pocket, accessed by a hand-and-toe trail of the ancients.

The Eagle Nest, hidden in an oval slit high above the ground, once accessed by a perilous traverse on Moqui steps that have now eroded away, epitomizes the defensive Pueblo III cliff dwelling.

As Vaughn and David can hardly swim a stroke, it was fortuitous that the San Juan River was at a low ebb that September of 2004.

A Navajo hogan, perhaps a century old, sits before the cliffs of the Comb.

Opposite page: *A dry, forbidding maze cuts west from the Comb, toward Cedar Mesa in the distance.*

A seldom-seen example of Pueblo III craftsmanship

Broken pottery tucked into a dry cave

Dunes blowing west across the Kane Valley on the Navajo reservation

Moqui steps leading up the steep western side of Comb Ridge. Dozens of known trails like this breach the cliffs of the Comb in its 120-mile length.

Near Kayenta, this complex of ruins greeted us within the first hours of the journey.

grim arroyo banks, the Chinle made up a gauntlet that would have defeated a seasoned mountain man.

Instead, we headed northwest across a flat plain, grazed to stubble by Navajo sheep, as we arrowed toward another spring marked on the map. Along the way, on various cliffs and boulders that we passed, we discovered more panels of rock art, all of them petroglyphs. Broad-shouldered Basketmaker humanoids prevailed, etched perhaps a thousand years or more before the Anasazi had turned into cliff dwellers: one dangling a chest pendant while she gave birth, another containing a miniature human entirely inside her torso—fetus or incubus? Bighorn sheep all over, one pierced with an atlatl dart. A dancer dangling snakes, mirrored by his upside-down reflection. A great long zigzag snake with forked tongue stabbing the air. Five flute players. Duck-headed humans holding hands and dancing, while the ducks themselves seemed to kiss each other. A string of human figures in profile running toward a fellow on his knees holding a crook-necked staff. The phantasmagoria of images was dazzling, and we would never know what any of it meant.

We reached the spring in a mere two hours. A pair of giant cottonwood trees sheltered this oasis in the desert. The spring had been modified into a well with a pump, a rusty iron plaque dating this improvement to 1969. Nearby stood the ruins of what looked to us like an old trading post. If so, it was the only Anglo building we would come across along the whole Comb Ridge. Inside, we found newspapers plastering the walls, dating from the 1940s. Who had built this lonely outpost? None of us had heard even a rumor of a trading post in this corner of the reservation.

As we ate lunch in the shade of the cottonwoods, suddenly three small dogs appeared on the brow of the hill above us to the west, barking fiercely but keeping their distance. Gradually a herd of sheep materialized, then, to the left, walking sideways as if to circle around us, a solitary human. It was instantly obvious that the sheepherder and his dogs were driving his flock, on this blisteringly hot day, toward the spring—but with us in occupation of the spot, they would not approach.

We grabbed some of the choice delicacies from our lunch—a fresh peach, a banana, and a cookie from our last resupply—and hurried up the hill to greet and apologize to the sheepherder. Slender and agelessly ancient, the man had a deeply creased visage under his beat-up Caterpillar cap. His eyes were fixed in a permanent squint against the sun and dust. He shook our hands with a limp grasp, then took our offerings, sat down on a rock, and turned the fruit over in his hands as though he had never seen a peach or a banana before. In true Navajo fashion, he avoided looking us in the eye.

We asked his name. "Maxie Platt," he answered in a voice as soft as a whisper. It soon became clear that he spoke only a few words of English. He did confirm that our presence was spooking the sheep and the dogs. "We'll get out of here," one of us said, "so you can take the sheep on down to the spring." Maxie did not even nod.

The meeting felt awkward in the extreme. Later Greg observed, "The poor guy seemed scared of us. Did you notice how he was shaking? I felt like I was accosting him, or trespassing on his ground."

At the time, I was oblivious to the nuances Greg picked up on. Now he and Vaughn were ready to take off, but, hungry for Navajo contact, I was determined to wring a scrap or two of local knowledge out of the old-timer. I pointed at the ruined trading post just below us. "Do you know who built it?"

Navajo sheepherder, Maxie Platt

"Lon Tanowa," answered Maxie in his soft voice. I scribbled the name in my journal.

As we hiked on into the north, I turned that cognomen over and over, like a pebble plucked from the seashore. *Lon Tanowa*—it didn't sound like either an Anglo or a Navajo name. Who was Lon Tanowa, and what was his story? After half an hour, the light dawned in my brain. What Maxie Platt had said was, "Long time ago." If he knew who had built the trading post, he wasn't telling me.

Just north of the spring, the Comb reasserted itself out of nowhere, in fierce and unclimbable 600-foot cliffs that swooped down to the sandy plain. If we were truly to follow the ridge here, we would have to head east down two miles of Chinle canyon—a stretch that Vaughn had found brutal even without a backpack—turn another corner, find a way to climb the lower cliffs on the west bank of the stream, hike two miles back to the crest, follow it for a mere two miles farther into the north, only to have to undo all that progress by climbing back down into the Chinle gorge again and finding a passage through it as it carved its way back toward the west.

The very prospect of such a labyrinthine ordeal seemed daunting, so we agreed, for once, to cheat. Across the next two and a half miles, we would skirt the Comb on the west. Cones of alkaline badlands, gray dirt heaps that parodied the slickrock we had hiked across for days, festooned the shallow valley through which we hiked. We crossed a low pass before heading downhill again.

In only an hour and a half, we had regained the Chinle where it burst through the gate it had carved in the Comb. Our shortcut had saved us five or six hours of miserable toil. Now we managed to splash across a riffled section of the chocolate stream with our boots on, but once we had climbed onto the bench on the far side, we could find no way up the smooth cliffs that arched toward the crest of the Comb, here only 200 feet above us.

Traversing back east as we sought an escape route, we ran smack into a geological nightmare—what I described in my journal as an "arroyo hole." Here, a small side-canyon had eroded so drastically that a thirty-foot-deep chasm blocked our way. In the end, leaving his pack on the bench, Greg managed to kick steps in the vertical mud, like an ice climber front-pointing down a waterfall pillar. When he reached an unstable platform, we broke out the rope and used it the only time we would on the entire traverse—in the inglorious task of

lowering our packs off that ugly precipice. By the time we had floun-
dered across the arroyo hole and out the far side, our faces and legs
and arms were coated with fine, brown dust.

Easy ramps led back to the crest of the Comb. We pushed on
till 5:00 PM, as cloudbanks amassed in the west and a stiff wind dried
our sweat. At last Vaughn threw down his pack on an arbitrary shelf,
indicating camp. We were carrying enough water to tide us through
dinner, breakfast, and the next day, but a little while after setting up
camp, Vaughn and I, out exploring on separate loops, each independently blundered upon the same generous tank full of water only
thirty yards from camp.

The glory of the canyons during the previous three days had spoiled
us. Here the Comb was grassy, scrubby, and inelegant, and the night
promised a windy bivouac. As I wrote in my journal, "Not a pretty
camp. Nondescript hollow in brownish-red dirt and bedrock. . . . Kind
of a down mood within the group."

That evening I looked over the maps. In nine days of backpacking
(with one of day hiking), we had covered sixty-six miles by foot, gaining fifty miles as the crow flies. The inescapable conclusion buoyed my
spirits. "Hey, guys," I said to Greg and Vaughn as we spooned down
our rehydrated macaroni and cheese, "we've covered half the Comb."

LEAVING THE REZ

ASIDE FROM ALL THE FOOD AND WATER, the sleeping bags, tents, and extra clothing, the pots and stove and fuel, Vaughn and Greg's camera gear, my book and my Crazy Creek chair—aside from all the stuff we were hauling in our backpacks, each of us was carrying his own less tangible baggage on the Comb Ridge.

As proprietor of Far Out Expeditions, the finest wilderness guide I had ever met had, in a sense, begun to paint himself into a professional corner. Each year the cost of Vaughn's overhead escalated—everything from vehicle repair and insurance on the three large four-wheel-drive vehicles he owned to permit fees for the BLM and the Navajo Nation (the latter for guiding Monument Valley and Mystery Valley tours) to the cost of gas and groceries. His profit margin, never robust to begin with, seemed to be shrinking with each season, even as his reputation spread and a cadre of loyal clientele returned for further outings. It was a measure of how much the Comb meant to him that Vaughn was willing to give up a month of bookings in predictably lucrative September to pursue our traverse.

Other guides, faced with just this dilemma, have made the logical corporate adjustment: they expanded their business, hired junior guides to lead the actual trips, and turned themselves from tour leaders into administrators. Several friends of Vaughn's and mine had gone from being river rats and climbing bums to settling back as fat-cat millionaires, by opting for this strategy. Such a course would have been anathema to Vaughn. Every trip on Cedar Mesa was an intimate personal journey for him, no matter who the clients. And to flood his beloved canyons with paying customers would have seemed flat-out immoral. Yet to pay the bills, at fifty-three Vaughn was still having to supplement his income during the off-season with construction work and contract archaeology.

Meanwhile, I had begun to detect in my friend not exactly the first signs of burnout, so much as a kind of chronic discouragement, exacerbated by his envy on those days when Greg and I got to scout some little-known canyon in Beef Basin while he led his umpteenth trip down Collins Canyon to the Narrows. On the Comb, I began to suspect that Vaughn's headlong charging off on his own vector—the kind of impetuous dash after the tamarisk bushwhack that had provoked our quarrel on September 7—was fueled by the fear that he would not get many more chances in life to undertake an extended journey of exploration for its own sake.

If so, that fear was reinforced by a physical setback that had plagued him throughout the previous year. For as long as I had known him, Vaughn had hiked the canyons not in boots, but in Chaco sandals, which he claimed were far more comfortable. Even with an eighty-pound pack on a weeklong trip with clients, he stuck to his sandals, and he had in fact become a sponsored representative for the Chaco company, based in Paonia, Colorado. At times I had wondered if there was a kind of machismo lurking beneath Vaughn's choice of footwear, for he plainly basked in his clients' awe at how he could stride through patches of prickly pear or cholla without stabbing his vulnerable toes, or stand around camp in a snowstorm with nothing warmer on his feet.

There's no getting around the fact, however, that sandals don't give you the arch support that boots do. And within the past year, Vaughn had begun to suffer from recurring pain in his arches, diagnosed by a doctor as full-on plantar fasciitis. With bitter resignation, Vaughn had started wearing his detested boots instead of his sandals, even beefing up the arch support with special insoles. And he had started taking large

During a previous reconnaissance of the Eagle Nest, Renée Globis peeks into the alcove.

doses of Vioxx. (Only a few weeks after our trip began, the company would take its wonder drug off the market, after clinical trials linked it to heart attacks and strokes.) As we set out on the Comb, then, Vaughn had serious doubts as to whether his feet would bear up under the strain of the longest backpack he had attempted in decades. By September 9, midway through our journey, he was overjoyed to find that his arches were giving him only the most minimal trouble.

Greg's baggage was of an utterly different kind. Two years before our trip began, he had gotten involved with Renée Globis, a pretty, superbly fit woman living in Moab. A 5.12 climber herself and an enthusiastic skier, mountain biker, hiker, and horseback rider, Renée seemed a perfect partner for Greg. Under Greg's, Vaughn's, and my tutelage, she too had been bitten by the Anasazi bug, so much so that she had planned to be the fourth member of our Comb Ridge team.

In November 2003, as they traveled in South Africa together while Greg researched an article for *Outside*, Renée got pregnant—a surprise for both herself and Greg. The baby was due in August, only weeks before our planned start on the Comb. Renée's sole major regret about this turn in her life was that it meant dropping out of our trip. I half expected Greg to drop out, too, but he pledged his determination to go ahead with the expedition, even if, should Renée's delivery come late, it might mean catching up with Vaughn and me several days into our trek.

Ariann Lucinda Child was born on August 9. Vaughn and I first saw the baby a couple of weeks later. She was a lovely, contented infant, with long strands of light brown hair. For all his tough-guy independence, Greg bonded with his daughter at once. I wondered if leaving her behind would vex our journey for him, but partway through our hike he said, "I didn't have the slightest qualms about going ahead with the trip. The kid'll be fine without me for a few weeks. And Renée's totally okay with this."

My own baggage had something to do with having turned sixty the year before. In 1993, for my fiftieth birthday, I'd had a big party, with friends flying in from as far away as Colorado. We'd played golf and soccer and touch football, drunk champagne and barbecued steaks, and showed slides of the exploits of our youth. For my sixtieth, however, in May 2003, I had wanted no fuss made. My wife, Sharon, and I went out for dinner—that was it. The evening passed for me in a gloomy funk.

The Comb Ridge seemed an answer of sorts to the fear that I was getting too old for the kinds of adventure that had anchored my life for the past four decades. The longest backpack I had ever attempted would not have quite the all-out commitment, the tiptoeing along the tightrope between life and death, that my most serious Alaskan climbing expeditions had required, but it would still be no mean accomplishment. During the previous year or two, on virtually every day hike on Cedar Mesa, as I exulted in the freedom of fast and efficient movement across the slickrock, I had been naggingly aware of how few such seasons in the outdoors might remain to me.

Those intimations of mortality had been given a darker tinge during the previous two years, as my sister, Jenny, three years younger than I, had contracted emphysema. In 1997, anticipating our mother's increasing frailty as she entered her eighties, Jenny had moved in with Mom in the house in which we had grown up in Boulder, to help take care of her. Instead, the tables had been turned, as Mom became Jenny's caretaker.

Jenny had quit smoking some twenty years before, but the emphysema not only progressed rapidly and drastically, it was punctuated with bouts of pneumonia that three times brought her close to sudden death. The Boulder and Denver doctors were at a loss to explain the virulence of Jenny's ailment. Finally, during a visit to the Mayo clinic in Scottsdale, Arizona, it was discovered that Jenny suffered from a rare protein deficiency in the lungs, called Alpha-1 Antitrypsin. The absence of that protein meant that any insult to the lungs—the cigarette smoke from two decades before—wreaked irreversible havoc. A congenital condition, the deficiency had to have been passed on to Jenny by one of our parents. It was the flip of a coin whether we children inherited the problem. I had myself tested and came out negative. Fate played its cruel hand here, for I had never smoked. I would gladly have accepted the deficiency myself in exchange for Jenny's health, but genes are indifferent to human wishes.

By the fall of 2003, Jenny had lost the job as a psychiatric social worker that she had loved and been proud to perform. She was on oxygen twenty-four hours a day. The last six months were hideous, as her condition spiraled downward. Several long hospital stays were succeeded by hospice. Terrified of dying in her sleep, she succumbed to panic every night as she started to nod off. Her two grown children, Scott and Kimberly, gave Jenny heroic support, as did my grief-stricken mother. But the single event Jenny tried to hang on to partake of—the birth of her granddaughter (Kimberly's child) in May—she would not be allowed to enjoy. Jenny died in hospice on March 6, 2004.

During one of my last visits to my sister, as I hugged her before heading out of her room at hospice, she said, with tears rolling down her cheeks, "You know, this really, really sucks!" I was too choked up to answer.

On the Comb Ridge, during the wee hours when I woke before dawn, I was aware of a vague malaise that hung over my spirit. Physically I felt great, in the best shape in years, sober as a Mormon, but there was no ignoring that faint though pervasive gloom. It took me almost two weeks, however, to put my finger on its linkage with Jenny's death, only six months before. But once I had, I kept hearing that cry of existential angst, full of knowledge of her doom—"This really sucks!"—echoing over and over in my head.

⚬⚬⚬

I had a bad night on September 9. A staccato patter of wind-blown rain forced me up after midnight to put the fly on the tent, yet in the morning I could see that the dusty squall had scarcely moistened the potholes near camp. In addition, my thin, half-length Therm-a-Rest pad had sprung a leak. I blew it up full twice during the night, only to have it deflate within an hour or so. In the morning, my bones ached from lying on the hardrock bulges underneath the tent. At the next resupply, I would swap the defective pad for the full-length (though twice as heavy) Therm-a-Rest I had used for years. Later, Vaughn's half-pad would also spring a leak.

We were off by 8:15 the next morning. Easy hiking on the relatively level crest of the Comb took us to yet another crossing of the Chinle, where the stream ostentatiously gouged its third gorge through the Cretaceous upthrust. In that canyon, Greg and Vaughn spotted a good Anasazi petroglyph panel a little ways upstream. We paused to admire and photograph it: a bighorn sheep with two smaller sheep inside its body, two guys with bows and arrows shooting at sheep, spirals of as many as twelve revolutions, and dancers raising their left arms in cryptic salutation. One dancer was stylized into a vertical quadrangle, right arm akimbo, left hand touching the top of his pseudo-head, legs spread to make room for a twin-lobed penis so long it dragged on the ground.

On the north side of the canyon, we climbed ramps back up toward the crest of the Comb. Here the Chinle meandered to the east, making sinuous bends that gave us glimpses of the tamarisk- and willow-thronged banks of the muddy stream. Down there, we spotted more wild burros, browsing on the leaves. And through his binoculars, Greg discovered a small ruin a mile ahead, tucked just under the caprock on the west rim of the canyon, another Pueblo III refuge all but invisible from afar.

We made a detour northeast to check it out. So well camouflaged was the ruin that twice we started scrambling below the rim in the wrong places before we identified the right caprock bulge. The ruin was nothing special, but a cunning craft had gone into its design, one L-shaped room wrapped around another, the whole barely large enough to house a single family. Fear and hard times in the thirteenth century, once again. . . .

We exited the site via the talus pile that sprawled beneath it. In the lead, I heard a sudden crashing noise behind me. I turned to witness what I thought, in that split second, was the catastrophe we had vaguely worried about for ten days, the casual mishap that could spell the demise of our whole expedition.

For the three or four hundredth time on the Comb, Greg had stepped on a boulder, this time one in the talus pile below the ruin. The big rock was loose, however, and it slid and then rolled under his weight. Greg fell awkwardly, slid himself, and then uttered a scream of pain.

Vaughn and I hurried to his side. Greg was cursing, both hands clutching his right ankle. He said later that his first thought was that the ankle was broken. In reality, it was badly sprained, but when he first tried to stand on it, he crumpled back to a sitting position, moaning with pain.

The scenario I had stored in the back of my head since the first day now played itself out on the screen of my imagination. Would we have to drag or carry Greg to the nearest patch of shade and leave him there, fortified with nearly all our water, while Vaughn and I hiked out to the nearest road? U.S. Highway 191, connecting Mexican Water in Arizona to the bridge five miles west of Bluff in Utah, lay only six miles east of us as the crow flies. What with finding a way down the cliffs in front of us, crossing the Chinle, climbing the opposite cliff, and then angling up to the Nokaito Bench and on across overgrazed badlands to the road, our mission would easily take half a day. Would we have to recruit a helicopter to come in and rescue Greg? I felt sick at heart.

There was always, of course, the sat phone. Such is the force of habit that the alternative scenario—sitting with Greg while we called in a chopper rescue—did not at once occur to me. Every mountaineer is imbued early on with the ethic that he has to get himself out of trouble. All three of us were proud that we had never had to be rescued in our lives.

Greg later told me there was no way he would have accepted a helicopter evacuation. "I once crawled off the top of El Cap," he recalled, "with a sprained ankle from a leader fall."

In case I needed further proof, now I bore witness to Greg's toughness. Vaughn fished out his medical kit and gave him a sturdy dose—800 milligrams—of ibuprofen. After twenty minutes, Greg said, "I think I can go on." He got back on his feet and hobbled across the talus and up to the rim. He hobbled, indeed, for the rest of the day, his pace about half what we had been maintaining that morning. Vaughn and I would surge ahead, and then stop and wait for our gimpy companion. Greg never complained. Despite steady infusions of ibuprofen, the ankle would bother him throughout the coming week, stiffening up in camp so that each morning's launch with his heavy backpack spelled a new ordeal. But from the moment he had said, "I think I can go on," Greg's resolve to finish the traverse never wavered.

Above us, only a mile to the northwest, loomed the Mule Ear. The closest thing the Comb boasts to a true pinnacle, this sharp, tilted slab forms a landmark that stands out for miles around. Vaughn and I had seen it many times, from Muley Point on the south end of Cedar Mesa, from farther north on the Comb, even from plateaus near Bluff. Vaughn had had a hankering to climb it for at least twenty

On the crest approaching the Mule Ear, with the San Juan River ahead

years. Though its summit, at a mere 5111 feet, is not even close to the highest point on Comb Ridge (that occurs on its extreme northern end, just before the ridge disintegrates into Whiskers Draw), the Mule Ear soars above its neighboring crests as does no other "tooth" in the whole hundred-mile-long massif.

From the low rim overlooking the Chinle, the Mule Ear loomed seven hundred feet above us, the last three hundred in the abrupt thrust of the pinnacle itself. Now, with Greg limping in the rear, we made our way slowly up toward that graceful spire. When we had almost reached its base, Vaughn, in the lead, rounded a small extrusion in the sandstone and ran smack into a bighorn sheep. Only seven or eight yards away, the animal—a mature male with a nearly full curl to its horns—jerked in startled fright and took off running downhill. We watched it as, trailing a cloud of dust, it clattered expertly across the slickrock and, in a matter of seconds, disappeared from view.

Vaughn could not contain his murmurs of surprise and joy. An erstwhile hunter of deer and elk, he had stopped going after big game many years ago; but he loved nothing more—not even perusing Anasazi rock art panels—than to watch animals in the wild. In 2001 on Edgeøya, the barren, uninhabited Svalbard island, we had stumbled upon a mature female polar bear. From a distance of 150 yards, our Norwegian guide had shot his flare gun. The charge exploded at the bear's feet; she had run a few yards away, and then stopped to peer at us in puzzled annoyance.

After that, as if already indifferent to our intrusion, the bear started cavorting on a snowbank. Overheated in the late-summer Arctic drizzle, in which we wore all our clothes to keep hypothermia at bay, the bear rolled down the snowbank again and again, in the process staining her white fur pink with the algae that resided in the snow. For an enthralled half hour, through our binoculars we watched this ursine play. Half an hour was enough for me, but Vaughn swore that he could have sat there watching all day. "There's nothing that gives me a bigger kick," he said.

Vaughn had never before come so close to a desert bighorn sheep in the wild. Both of us had seen sheep on the San Juan River, a few miles upstream from Mexican Hat. That small band, in fact, lingered so regularly at certain bends in the river that the rafting companies could almost guarantee sightings on their one-day floats from Bluff to Mexican Hat. Yet it is characteristic for male bighorns to go off on long solo excursions. The sheep we had spooked here could well have belonged to the San Juan herd.

We tackled the Mule Ear by its south ridge, only to be turned back in the face of a dangerously exposed, nearly vertical arête. Even with a good ankle, Greg would have had to summon up uncanny nerve to solo that ridge, and if he did, he would have found no safe anchor from which to belay Vaughn and me.

Finally we assaulted the Mule Ear from the east, frictioning flat-footed up its smooth (and likewise exposed) forty-five-degree slabs. The terrain reminded me of the Flatirons above Boulder, where I had done my first technical climbing at the age of seventeen. Taking three separate routes, we arrived on top within minutes of each other, and then sat wolfing down a lunch of sardines in mustard sauce, crackers, gorp, and energy bars, as we stared at the limitless vistas to the west.

By 3:00 that afternoon, we had traversed another two miles of the Comb, hiking effortlessly across a level bench just east of the crest. We were now within two air miles of the San Juan River, which indeed we had seen snaking into view north of us from the summit of the Mule Ear. Vaughn spotted a series of sizable potholes full of water in the distance and declared the place an ideal campsite. Normally I would have agreed with him, but on one of my May reconnaissance trips I had discovered, just a mile to the northeast of where we now stood, what I considered a matchless place to pitch our tents.

I had hiked in from the east, down a short, unnamed side-canyon of the Chinle, to investigate yet another spring marked on the map. What I had found was a generous fountain of clear, pure water seeping out of the cattails a few hundred yards above the side-canyon's mouth. There was a level bench for our tents, a slickrock basin on which to lounge beside the flowing spring and to cook our dinner and breakfast.

As seemed to happen so regularly on our trip, the decision as to where to pitch camp spurred a debate between Vaughn and me that edged toward the acrimonious. With my memory of the spring and the side-canyon shelves so vivid in my head, I was determined not to give in. At last Vaughn acquiesced.

We scrambled down into the canyon of the Chinle and crossed, barefoot, the gooey, slippery stream for the fifth time. (Eventually we would ford the Chinle a total of sixteen times.) By 4:00 PM we were installed beside the spring. Greg and Vaughn reluctantly admitted that it was a near-perfect campsite. The flow of water was so prodigal that

Roberts reading from Traders to the Navajo

we kept an upper pool for drinking, a lower one, in which we could sit neck-deep, for lolling naked and bathing for the only time during our trip. Fresh from his ablutions, Greg cracked, "I was wondering if it was Vaughn's feet I was smelling, but it was my own tee shirt."

It was not our most spectacular campsite—that would remain the high shelf with the five giant potholes where we had passed the night of September 6–7. But it would prove to be our coziest and most idyllic. And once again, we would take a layover day here, leaving our tents pitched in the morning so we could prowl in all directions, carrying only our day packs, as we searched for yet more ruins and rock art.

The decrepit trading post beside the spring, where we had run into the ageless sheepherder Maxie Platt on September 9, had lodged in my consciousness. Meanwhile, each night I was continuing to read Gillmor's *Traders to the Navajos*, which gave me a vivid picture of the lonely and dangerous enterprise of running such an outpost at the beginning of the twentieth century.

Even before John Wetherill set out for Oljato, he was warned against the journey by Navajos at Chinle and Chaco Canyon. "Don't go," they said. "There are bad people there. They will kill you." Unfazed, the cowboy from Mancos, Colorado, saddled up and rode into that outback, so little known to Anglos. In March 1906, he arrived at Oljato—the Place of Moonlight Water in the Diné tongue—where he was met by a stern-faced Navajo headman on horseback, escorted by four armed men (Wetherill, a Quaker, traveled unarmed). The headman told the intruder to turn around and go home. Instead, Wetherill held his ground and insisted on talking. Then, in a stroke of genius— premeditated, one wonders, or spontaneous?—he proposed a rabbit feast. "You get the rabbits," he said to the Navajos, "and I'll furnish flour and sugar and coffee."

Three days later, the Navajos and Wetherill sat around a fire eating roast rabbit and fresh-baked bread, while they drank coffee sweetened with sugar. The Navajos, in this remote corner of the reservation, were not easily persuaded of the advantages of letting a trader settle in their midst. "We have lived all this time without white men here," said one elder. "It is our country. We want no white men here."

Wetherill kept talking. (Did an acculturated Navajo translate—for at the time, Wetherill spoke little or no Diné? Did they converse in Spanish, as was often the practice in the early days of Anglo-Navajo contact? Gillmor is silent on the question.) He pointed out the advantages of trade. The coffee and bread—almost unheard-of luxuries for the Navajo who lived far from the nearest white settlements—worked their magic.

Thirty miles west of Oljato stands Navajo Mountain, an isolated, broad-shouldered dome sacred to the Diné that soars to an altitude of 10,388 feet. The canyons on all sides of the great peak form one of the most rugged and most beautiful wildernesses in all the Southwest. Even today, that region is seldom visited by Anglos. By 1906 it is possible that no white man had yet penetrated its labyrinth—unless some unrecorded prospector or trapper on the Colorado had boldly pushed his way up one of the several side-canyons that make their tortuous passages from the slopes of Navajo Mountain down to the great river.

All this country was the domain of Hoskinini, by 1906 an old man, but revered as one of the greatest of all the leaders of the Diné. The headman who had first ordered Wetherill out of the country was one of Hoskinini's sons. In 1863 and 1864, as Kit Carson, with his murderous Ute allies, had tried to round up all the Navajos and send them on the Long Walk to Bosque Redondo, Hoskinini had rallied a large contingent of men, women, and children and led them into the natural stronghold on the slopes of Navajo Mountain. Carson had chased this band to the banks of the San Juan River, where he gave up in dismay at the roughness of the country ahead.

Through the next five years, until the grim and lethal Bosque Redondo concentration camp was finally declared a failure and the Navajos were freed to return to their homeland, Hoskinini hid out with his people, eking out a living on roots and piñon nuts and stray sheep that Carson's troops had overlooked. The chief was legendary for his generosity, nursing the poorest and sickliest of his charges back to health. And when their relatives returned in 1868 from their imprisonment in eastern New Mexico, Hoskinini's band could take immense pride in the fact that they had weathered the genocidal mass removal as some of the only Navajo who had never been captured or enslaved. No wonder, then, that at first they wanted no part of a trading post at Oljato.

Slowly, however, Wetherill won over the dubious Navajos sitting beside the fire, who were impressed by the cowboy's bravery at riding unarmed into this Anglo no-man's-land. "It is far to Round Rock," Wetherill said, naming the trading post just north of Canyon de Chelly—"ninety miles to take your wool and skins. It is seventy miles to Red Lake, eighty miles to Bluff. A long way to ride for flour to cook bread like this." At last, Hoskinini himself gave his blessing.

Within weeks of building the trading post, Louisa Wetherill had started to learn the Diné tongue. A natural polyglot, she mastered the difficult language in relatively short order, as her husband never would. Hoskinini was so astonished at Louisa's fluency in Diné that he became convinced she must be his granddaughter, the direct descendant of a beloved wife who had been captured by the Utes many years before and never seen again. After all, Louisa came from the Ute country (Mancos), and how else could she speak the people's tongue virtually without an accent, unless she had learned it from her grandmother?

For the rest of his life, Hoskinini called Louisa "granddaughter." When he died in 1909, he bequeathed her his thirty-two Ute women slaves. Louisa tried to set the women free, but they were unwilling to go. Instead, she made sure they were fed, built them a hogan of their own, and gave them useful chores to do when they begged to be put to work.

An avid botanist, Louisa set out to memorize the Navajo names of all the local plants and to learn about their medicinal uses. (The sum of this incomparable lore, consigned by Louisa to detailed notebooks, has never been published.) And, through an elderly man named Wolfkiller, who had heard the stories from his own mother, Louisa gained extraordinary insights into the Navajo past, as handed down by oral tradition.

During our last few days along the Chinle, mixed in with the dazzling Anasazi sites we had discovered, we found plenty of signs of the early Navajo, mainly in the form of old sweat lodges and hogans. Once more, I pondered long and hard about the relationship between those two so different peoples. Now, in Gillmor's pages, I read Wolfkiller's stories of the Old Ones, as he passed them on to Louisa Wetherill. Some of these strange gleanings puzzled me to the edge of incredulity.

Louisa had asked the elder what certain Anasazi rock art panels might signify. Wolfkiller was extremely reluctant to talk about the petroglyphs and pictographs, for, in the Navajo way of thinking, even to remember past calamities was to risk inflicting them upon the living all over again. "That is why we do not speak of the writing on the rocks," Wolfkiller explained. "Most of them concern troubles of long ago, and we must not bring them again upon our people."

The single passage that most disturbed—and at the same time, fascinated—me had to do with Navajo legends about the Tsegi canyons, just west of Kayenta, not far from where we had started our Comb traverse. In Wolfkiller's telling, the Navajo had coexisted for a long time in the Southwest with another people who "lived in stone houses under the cliffs, because they were afraid of some of the tribes who made raids upon them from time to time." Calling these people the Tsegi-Etso, the Navajo had watched as they moved into the Tsegi and built some of their grandest cliff dwellings, including Betatakin and Keet Seel—today, the two most impressive Anasazi ruins in Arizona. Both names are in fact Navajo, meaning "ledge house" and "broken pottery," respectively. Today's Hopi call those ancestral ruins by quite other names—*Talastima* (place of the corn tassel) instead of Betatakin, *Tokonav* (place of the black rock) instead of Keet Seel. Richard Wetherill, John's oldest brother, had made the Anglo discovery of Keet Seel in 1895, but in his trek up the Tsegi, he had completely missed Betatakin, tucked away in a short side-canyon, leaving John to discover the stunning ruin in 1909, when he was guided there by a young Navajo.

According to Wolfkiller, then, the Navajo had been around early enough to watch the Anasazi go into the Tsegi system and build those peerless villages, each guarded by the massive alcove that enclosed it. "Everything went well for some time," Wolfkiller reported. But then a prolonged drought struck, and after the rains returned, great windstorms ravaged the land, knocking over trees. As the old man told Louisa,

> *By this time the people in the canyons were very weak. They were trying to live, but they had married into their own families and there were many blind, deaf, and hunchbacks among them. They were getting too weak to fight for their existence.*

> *There came a time when there were snakes moving everywhere. The people from the different houses at last came together. There were very few of them left by this time. They decided the canyons were bewitched and prepared to move.*

> *Our people had been moving around the country from place to place all of this time, but they were near the Tsegi when the people came out.*

According to Wolfkiller, those wretched refugees from the Tsegi made their way south across Black Mesa, where they founded the town of Oraibi—confirming their role as ancestors of the Hopi, who still live in Oraibi on the Third Mesa today.

This visionary passage seemed to me impossible to reconcile with the archaeology of the Southwest. When Gillmor was writing, in the early 1930s, anthropologists had yet to fix a likely date for the first entry into the Southwest of the Navajo from the subarctic north. Nor had the cliff dwellings yet been firmly dated.

In a tour de force of tree-ring dating carried out by Jeffrey Dean in the 1960s, the scholar demonstrated that Betatakin had been built and abandoned in the strikingly brief span between 1267 and some time very shortly after 1286. Keet Seel, on the other hand, had been occupied as early as 950, although the ruin that stands today—a magnificent complex of some 160 rooms, the largest cliff dwelling in Arizona—was started only around 1250. Forty years after Dean's pioneering work, with hundreds of thousands of Anasazi roof beams now precisely dated, no one has found a single cutting date anywhere in the vast abandonment region later than 1286, the date given by a single beam each at Betatakin and Keet Seel. The Tsegi canyons seem to have been the last place the Old Ones hung on at the end of the thirteenth century, before launching their mass migration to the south and east.

Most scholars now believe that the Navajo could not have arrived in the Southwest before about 1500. Wolfkiller's old stories, however, would push that advent back by a minimum of two and a half centuries, and maybe much longer. I was thus tempted to dismiss those stories as mere fairy tales—perhaps as parables retrospectively invented to explain the demise of a people with powerful magic who had gone grievously wrong, whose empty ruins the Navajo had been startled to find when they first moved into the Southwest. (In this respect, the tales were like the strictures upon the vanished Anasazi, with their powerful magic that they ultimately abused, tendered to Robert McPherson by his Navajo informants on the reservation in the 1980s.) Yet there was such a haunting sense of immediacy about Wolfkiller's stories, such an apparent authenticity of witness, that it was hard to reject them out of hand.

It would not be until several weeks after our Comb trip that an archaeologist friend—the brilliant Stephen Lekson of the University of Colorado—offered me an escape route from this prehistoric paradox. Even by the time of Wolfkiller's mother's girlhood, say around 1820 or 1830, there had been considerable intermarriage between Pueblo people and Navajo. Descendants of those long-ago couplings might well, by 1910, identify themselves as entirely Navajo. Yet they carried in their heads, as well as in their genes, the legacy of the people who had indeed built and abandoned Betatakin and Keet Seel. Wolfkiller himself may have had a great-great-great-grandparent who had fled the Four Corners in the thirteenth century as the only solution to an environmental and perhaps spiritual catastrophe. Old tales die hard.

———— ∞∞∞ ————

From the bench below the Mule Ear, only an hour before Greg had sprained his ankle, we had spotted one of the strangest ruins any of the three of us had ever seen in the Southwest. The temptation was to drop everything and head for it, but it lay on the far side of the Chinle, across a canyon whose steep cliffs on both sides could have taken a long time to negotiate. Instead, we agreed to save it for the morrow, our "rest day," when we would leave camp pitched beside the abundant spring in the cozy side-canyon.

On September 11, carrying only day packs, we got off at 8:15 AM, anticipating a quick trip back to the strange ruin, which now lay three miles up the Chinle. The going proved much harder than we expected, as awkward cliffs forced us to cross the Chinle twice. Between devious scrambling, nasty bushwhacking, broad patches of poison ivy to avoid, and thigh-deep quicksand to wade through in the stream itself, the second crossing took a full hour from rim to rim—even though during that thrash we descended and regained a mere hundred feet of altitude and covered a horizontal distance of less than a quarter-mile.

Thus it took us almost three hours to wend our way back upstream to the anomalous ruin—but what a reward for our toil! So far along the Chinle, virtually every Anasazi ruin we had found had been a cliff dwelling. Here, however, the ruin stood out in the open, bare to the sky, on a peninsula of bedrock thrusting west where the stream below made a sharp bend. The "Fortress," as I began calling it, was a massive, D-shaped enclosure built right to the edge of the 120-foot precipice that plunged sheer to the Chinle. Most open-air pueblos crumble over the centuries, leaving little more than tumbledown piles of stones from which archaeologists must deduce the shape of the former village. The Fortress, however, had been so well built that it preserved its shape largely intact. The walls themselves, expertly masoned with fitted chunks of red tabular sandstone, were an unfathomable two and a half feet thick. At their tallest, those walls soared ten feet high. Yet there was no evidence that the structure had ever had a roof—no collapsed timbers inside to indicate roof beams.

Everything about the ruin was massive. The long axis of the D was forty-five feet, the short axis twenty-one. Inside, Vaughn thought he could detect the vestiges of a roomblock or two, with maybe a rudimentary kiva, but the predominant fact about the building was that it made a giant enclosure that could have sheltered a small throng, and that would have been extremely difficult to attack. Small doorways opened into the enclosure on either end of the D, but its defensive aura was heightened by the absence of a single window. Instead, nine loopholes or peepholes pierced the walls, well-crafted tubes through which the inhabitants—the refugees?—might have spied on enemies arriving from farther east on the bedrock peninsula.

The Fortress defied what we knew about the norms of Anasazi architecture. As I wrote in my journal, "I've never seen anything like it. It's one of the largest Anasazi enclosures of any kind I've ever seen in the backcountry. . . . What was it?!"

Yet the Fortress was only part of a prehistoric complex. Just below the rim on which the enclosure stood, a row of small cliff dwellings and granaries occupied every square foot of a fragmentary ledge. By hiking east along the cliff edge to a protruding point, we could study those huddled structures with our binoculars but could see no way to climb into them. Greg would eventually devote hours to the effort, circling far afield to scramble down to the Chinle itself, and then trying to find a route up to the secretive buildings. Eventually he gained the easternmost of the structures and tried to crawl along the ledge to gain the central and more interesting sector of the ruins. As he later told Vaughn and me, invoking the jargon of the rock climber, "It was like a horizontal off-width with the edge right here." He made

Like a medieval castle, this sturdy D-shaped keep overlooked the Chinle Wash on the Navajo reservation.

a vigorous slicing motion with his left hand that skimmed his hip. "I inched forward, then I said no, then I inched, then no. I looked at the ruin beyond the crawlway with my binocs. It's really well preserved. But it was too scary to push."

In all likelihood, then, here was a ruin that no one had reached in the last seven centuries, since the last inhabitants had packed up and left for good. Right away, however, we had discovered the one plausible means of access to the central sector of cliff dwellings. From the very middle of the Fortress, a well-placed log ladder, inclined near the dead vertical, might barely have reached the ledge below. That would have meant a terrifying daily ascent and descent, one misstep sending the hapless denizen to a hundred-foot fall and certain death. Even the rope we carried was useless to gain access to the hidden cliff dwellings, for there was nothing to tie it to to anchor a rappel.

After some two hours spent admiring the Fortress, Vaughn and I took off on a long loop back toward camp, circling high among the eastern cliffs to check out several alcoves that looked like Basketmaker caves. The going was consistently arduous: ledges that blanked out in sheer slabs, brutal thickets of scrub oak and swaths of poison ivy blocking the alcove mouths. Eventually we scrambled into three such caves, finding Basketmaker cists, a pair of *manos* (grinding stones) made of white river cobbles, perfectly preserved corncobs that were at least 1500 years old, grooves in the bedrock boulders where the ancients may have sharpened their tools, and a few minimalist petroglyphs and painted handprints.

The temperature was still hovering in the 90s. Back in camp, worn out after our eight-hour push ("rest day" indeed!), Vaughn and I lolled joyously in our bathing pool as we traded theories about what the Fortress might have meant—signal tower? Kiva enclosure? Redoubt to guard the only route into the cliff dwellings below? Greg, who had stayed on the west side of the Chinle all day, didn't get back to camp until 6:20 PM, a little before dusk, just as I was starting to worry about him. He'd made his own discoveries, the finest of which was an airy scramble up an eroded Anasazi hand-and-toe trail to a complex of dwellings that completely filled an elongated oval aperture in the cliff, eighty feet off the deck. Once more, in the front walls of the buildings he found loopholes but no windows.

The whole of the Chinle seemed to reverberate with the terror of the thirteenth century. As I had often reflected after visits to other late

Ruins above Chinle Wash

Pueblo III cliff dwellings, it was at the same time beguiling and unsettling to see how the fear that had ruled the daily lives of the Old Ones had transmuted over the ages into the beauty of the failed strongholds they had left behind.

We got one of our earliest starts yet on the morning of September 12. Only two air miles from the San Juan, we were eager to cross the river and leave the Navajo Reservation behind. Yet I felt a kind of regret, too, about that looming transition in our long trek. By that morning, we had hiked some seventy-nine miles in eleven days, gaining at least sixty as the crow flies, completing three-fifths of our journey. I knew that the country we were leaving behind was by far the least-visited sector of Comb Ridge. And I was quite sure that the forty-some miles north of the San Juan would not compare in archaeological richness to the terrain in which we had luxuriated during the previous five days, where the Chinle snaked back and forth through the Comb, carving a landscape that had once been an Anasazi paradise.

There were plenty of ruins and rock art panels along the stretch of the Comb ahead, but Vaughn and I had already visited many of those sites on day hikes out of Butler Wash. The thrill of discovery through the remainder of our trip would inevitably be muted by comparison with the glorious days behind us.

Almost a week earlier, as we had approached our second resupply, where the dirt road traversed the Comb, Greg had pointed out that we had yet to see a single footprint in six days of hiking. There were footprints beside the road, of course, where Jim Hook had handed us provisions and gear for the upcoming stretch. But then we had hiked for another five and a half days without spotting a single footprint.

Now, however, just a few hundred yards below the camp of the gushing spring, we saw footprints—sandal tracks, from boaters on the San Juan who had pulled to shore at the mouth of the Chinle and had hiked up its banks. Vaughn and I had performed just such jaunts ourselves, and so the sites we now passed were not new to us, though they were to Greg. Still, I was dazzled all over again by the variety of this last canyon corridor of the Chinle. In the east-facing cliff, only thirty-five feet up (reached prehistorically no doubt by a log ladder), stood a handsome row of dwellings, several made out of daub-and-wattle (mud and sticks cleverly woven into lightweight lattices in lieu of stone-masoned walls). The caprock above the diminutive village overhung so fiercely that if you rappelled off it, you'd be dangling in space fifteen feet out from the ledge on which the buildings stood.

To the left of that ruin was a famous pictograph, nicknamed Baseball Man. What looked at first glance like a single composition was actually two, executed centuries apart. A classic Basketmaker anthropomorph in white paint, broad shoulders, hands dangling at its sides, ear bobs prominent, had been superimposed by a late Pueblo "shield" symbol—a white-and-red spheroid in which the twin curving lines of "stitches" uncannily resembled the horsehide cover of a baseball. When I had first looked at this pictograph in 1994, Polly Schaafsma, the rock art expert along on our float trip, had mused that the "baseball" might be a hex sign, an ominous warning to visitors to go away or perhaps a spell cast on the spirits of the distant ancestors who had limned the humanoid that the hex half-obliterated. In recent years, however, Schaafsma had changed her thinking about shield symbols, seeing them as images evocative not only of real shields but of such supernatural beings as the Puebloan War Twins. Why the shield might be superimposed on the far earlier anthropomorph was still anybody's guess.

Only a few yards north of Baseball Man was another striking pictograph, one Vaughn had nicknamed Walking Star. In its entirety, the design, painted in white, amounted to a circular, headless torso atop legs and feet marching to the right. Inside the torso, a five-pointed star floated in some kind of immanent limbo.

Downstream two hundred yards on the other side of the canyon, along a cliff band facing west, we perused a crowded petroglyph panel. Two duck-headed humanoids were fighting each other with atlatls. Hunchbacked "burden carriers"—backpackers like us?—slouched toward the San Juan. A spiral unfurled toward a Basketmaker figure with huge hands held aloft. A flute player lay on his back, legs kicked up in apparent ecstasy. Pregnant with lost meaning, the panel tantalized us like all the others we had found during the previous twelve days.

At last we burst out of the Chinle canyon, traversed a high bench,

Baseball Man consists of overlapping paintings by Basketmaker and later Pueblo artists.

and came to the south shore of the San Juan. We had scheduled Jim Hook's arrival on the far bank, with his "rubber ducky" rafts in tow, for 10:30 AM, still two hours away. The near bank was a steep talus pile abutting the Comb itself, so jumbled it was hard to find a decent place to sit down. We gazed across sixty or seventy yards of swift-moving current, almost as chocolate in hue as the Chinle. The north bank of the river gave way to a solid jungle of Russian olive trees. The rendezvous point, we knew (Vaughn had been there), was where a rutted dirt road that trundled down Comb Wash ended in a cottonwood grove. That location was sometimes used as a put-in or take-out spot for rafters, but the Russian olives were so thick and tall that we couldn't gauge just where the grove was. We began to imagine an absurd scenario in which Jim fought his way with his rubber duckies through the thicket to a shore too far up- or downstream for us to see him.

Greg volunteered to swim the river without his pack, plunge through the thorny jungle, and intercept Jim as he wheeled down the old road. Vaughn and I were relieved. I myself had never learned to swim, and water that came much above my thighs tended to terrify me—though in counterphobic spasms of denial, I had signed aboard expeditions to New Guinea and Ethiopia with expert rafters trying to make the first descents of two wilderness rivers. Vaughn could accomplish a thrashing crawl in a swimming pool, but he was not much more sanguine about rivers or lakes than I. Greg, on the other hand, was a powerful swimmer with no fear of water.

The more we stared at the San Juan, the more we realized that its flow was at relatively low volume. It had scarcely rained during the previous eight days, and the flood that had swelled the river to 13,000 cubic feet per second on September 4 had ebbed steadily each day thereafter. Would it even be possible to wade the San Juan?

On his first try, angling slowly across sand bars invisible in the muddy water, Greg got most of the way to the far shore before the current rose to his neck. He half-hopped, half-swam the rest of the way, as Vaughn and I hallooed our congratulations. Still, there was no way we could get our packs across such a ford.

Returning toward our bank, Greg tried a passage about a hundred yards farther downstream. Here, amazingly, he went in no more than waist-deep. He had discovered the ford that would take us across without the use of rubber duckies!

Even with a stout branch as a walking pole, I edged into the swift current with trepidation. "Greg, if I lose it, you can save me, right, huh?" I blurted out. Greg just laughed.

Step by cautious step, we inched our way across the river behind Greg. Exultation trumped my anxiety. I whooped with excitement. Lapsing, as he sometimes did, into the portentous tones of a voice-over narrator annotating the documentary film of our voyage, Greg proclaimed, "Were it not for Child's mastery of the river, we should all surely have perished."

I was still whooping with joy as we staggered onto the muddy north bank of the San Juan. At once, Greg found a cow path through the Russian olives. We clumped through that tunnel in the green jungle to emerge smack at the cottonwood grove. Tossing off our heavy packs, we lay full-length on the ground to wait for the now unnecessary rubber duckies.

"I sure hope Jim remembers to bring some of that you-know-what," I ventured.

"You can say it now," Greg rejoined.

"Yeah." I blinked. "Beer! We're off the rez!"

THE COMB GETS ROUGH

WHERE WE HAD CROSSED THE SAN JUAN, we were at an altitude of 4200 feet, the lowest point on our whole traverse. Through the next forty miles (as the crow flies), we would tread a gauntlet of endless ups and downs, with a bit more up than down, as the Comb, in erratic fits, swooped to an altitude of 6600 feet just before expiring in Whiskers Draw.

Punctual as always, Jim Hook arrived at 10:40 on the morning of September 12. Instead of the truck he had used for his previous resupplies, he was driving the vehicle he fondly called Big Yellow, a low-geared Polaris that looked something like an overgrown golf cart but that could handle roads that would defeat most four-wheel-drive vans or SUVs. As he bounced into view from around a corner to the north, Jim presented an almost comic spectacle, the pair of inflated yellow rubber duckies lashed atop the bright yellow cart.

In the passenger seat rode Marcia, Vaughn's wife. Their reunion was a heartfelt one, as they hugged for long moments, for despite Vaughn's guiding, it was rare for the couple to be apart for as long as twelve days. (Into our previous resupplies, Marcia had stowed cards scrawled with loving messages. Vaughn would pause in his repacking, move away from us to read his wife's note, and then scribble down his own endearments for Jim to carry back to Marcia.)

Jim told us that the San Juan was indeed low, even for mid-September, running at only 400 cfs. If he was disappointed that our ford of the river had precluded his heroic mission of ferrying us across in the duckies, he didn't let on. I seized the sports section of *USA Today*. The Red Sox still trailed the Yankees, but they were six games ahead in the wild-card race. I sighed. Perhaps there was still a faint hope of revenge in the American League Championship Series. Aaron Boone's home run in the eleventh inning of the seventh game the year before, giving the hated Yanks their nail-biting triumph, was still seared in my brain.

Jim must have noticed the dubious look I gave his souped-up golf cart, for now he patted Big Yellow and said, "This is the Willys Jeep of my middle age." Then he pulled a cooler out of the backseat and opened it. I saw red cans of precious Tecate, beaded with icy sweat. Eleven in the morning seemed a bit early for the cocktail hour, but Greg and I each seized a can and popped the top. Vaughn, puritan to the end, declined.

I took a medium-sized swig, then blurted out, "God, does that taste good!" Greg and I clinked cans. But after downing my first beer in twelve days, I was actually dizzy. Nothing, I thought, would feel better than a nice nap, curled up here in the dirt of the cottonwood grove. But we had San Juan Hill to climb, a 500-foot-high rib where the Comb resumed in earnest, looming directly above us. Glancing at that rise, Jim chuckled and said, "I'm sure glad I don't have to carry a heavy pack up that hill."

Even in the cottonwood shade, it was still an alarmingly warm morning. Jim mentioned that during the previous week, the temperature had climbed as high as ninety-five degrees in Bluff. "There's supposed to be a twenty percent chance of rain on Wednesday," he said, trying to cheer us up. But Wednesday was three days away.

This mission in Big Yellow did not qualify as a bona fide resupply, though we filled our bottles with water from Jim's five-gallon jug. Only three miles north of our cottonwood grove, State Highway 163 cut its ruthless, dynamite-sculpted notch through the Comb. We would leisurely make our way across those three miles, descend to the highway, and meet Marcia in the late afternoon. She was bringing the goods in a Far Out Expeditions van, a mere six-mile jaunt from her home in Bluff, for our next four-day stretch. With her would come

Renée, who had driven down from Castle Valley for the reunion, and Ariann, now officially one month and three days old.

We hoisted our packs, said goodbye to Jim and Marcia, and started up San Juan Hill. I was still slightly blotto from the Tecate. Somehow the effort of hiking uphill seemed more onerous than ever, with the blazing noonday sun on our shoulders.

Almost at once, we struck the grade of a faint track that snaked its way up the ridge, and in doing so, stepped into history. For here, the last great obstacle in one of the most astounding pilgrimages in Western history had been overcome. A century and a quarter later, that pilgrimage still had the capacity to inspire awe.

In 1847 Brigham Young arrived with his Mormon emigrants in the Great Salt Lake Basin, where he famously decreed, "This is the place." Year after year of subsequent migrations swelled the burgeoning colony, until by 1855 it numbered more than 40,000 men, women, and children. The utopian settlement's success led Young and other Mormon leaders to flaunt their polygamy openly and to declare a de facto independence from the United States. In 1857 an incensed President James Buchanan sent 2500 soldiers to Utah to restore federal law to the breakaway kingdom of Latter-day Saints. It was the paranoid climate of that impending confrontation that launched the Mountain Meadows Massacre on September 11, 1857, when Mormons attacked a California-bound emigrant train near St. George, Utah, and in a matter of minutes killed 120 of their number in cold blood, including 20 women and 50 children—by far the worst such massacre in American history.

The continuing enmity between Mormons and non-Mormons through the 1860s and 1870s prompted Young to send out missions to all of the surrounding territories, to found Mormon enclaves from Colorado to Idaho, Wyoming to Arizona, and even in the Mexican states of Chihuahua and Sonora. (These latter *colonias*, still Mormon towns today, were conceived of by Young as the vanguard of a possible mass relocation of all the Saints out of the United States and its territories, should federal opposition to the practice of polygamy provoke a war.)

Brigham Young died in 1877, but the colonizing movement proceeded apace. By that year, news of miners and cattle ranchers creeping from Colorado into the southeast corner of Utah Territory had reached the ears of the Mormon leaders in Salt Lake. It was to keep the Gentiles (as the Saints called all non-Mormon whites) out of that corner of Utah that the Hole-in-the-Rock expedition was born.

In April 1879, a scouting party of twenty-six men, two women, and eight children set out from Paragonah, a hamlet near Cedar City in southwestern Utah. It took this team six weeks to make a long loop south through Arizona, crossing the Colorado River at Lee's Ferry, a few miles below today's Glen Canyon Dam. The hardest part of the journey was the trudge across the desert from the Indian village of Moenkopi through the badlands of northeastern Arizona, across the Chinle, and north to the San Juan. Here, the explorers often struggled for twenty miles or more between fetid water holes.

And here, they felt much threatened by Navajos. One diarist recorded a not atypical encounter:

This Indian would kick the dirt on our food, and struck our knife blades on the rocks. He would draw his knife across his throat to show my wife and children what he would do to them when he got help. Our boys acted like the time had come for them to kill or be killed. I begged them not to fire the first shot.

The scouting party managed to push through to the San Juan without a pitched battle, but they arrived with a vivid sense of the danger of intruding upon the Navajo homeland. On the San Juan, the explorers spent two and a half months trying to determine the ideal location for their new Mormon stronghold, finally settling on the site of today's Montezuma Creek. They eventually completed their thousand-mile reconnaissance by following a much easier loop to the north, more or less along the path of today's Highway 191 and Interstates 70 and 15, returning at last to Paragonah in mid-September.

A month later, the colonizing expedition—230 men, women, and children in eighty-three wagons, accompanied by a thousand horses and cattle—set out from Cedar City. Daunted by the scouts' tales of debilitating thirst and Navajo hostility in northeastern Arizona, the colonists rejected out of hand the idea of following the southern loop that their predecessors had blazed. By far the most logical itinerary would have been to backtrack along the northern loop by which the scouting party had returned. Yet for some reason, the leaders of the colonizing mission decided to forge a "shortcut" straight east of Cedar

City, across terrain virtually no white men had ever explored—a decision that David E. Miller, the definitive historian of the Hole-in-the-Rock expedition, says "has never been fully explained."

The party carried six weeks' worth of provisions. The desperate journey would ultimately require six months.

The farthest outpost of Mormon settlement east of Cedar City was the small town of Escalante, founded in 1875. Beyond that lonely ranching community stretched a wilderness that only a handful of Paiutes and Navajos knew well. Some of the Escalante ranchers had started grazing their sheep and cattle a little ways out into the badlands, but even they seemed intimidated by its barren emptiness—an aura that lingers in the name the locals still use to allude to that endless bench of sand dunes and bedrock: the Desert.

It was early November 1879 when the Hole-in-the-Rock expedition passed through Escalante. There the pilgrims purchased their last additional stores of potatoes, sorghum, and flour—every ounce of which would prove vital to survival. With the leaders forging ahead to build a crude road to accommodate the wagons, the team made painfully slow progress. By the end of November, the massive party was ensconced at a place they called Forty-mile Spring—forty miles southeast of Escalante. (Fortymile Gulch, a handsome canyon tributary to the Escalante River, preserves that pioneer appellation.)

By now the first snows of winter had fallen, effectively cutting the team off from retreat to Escalante. Six weeks had passed since leaving Cedar City, and the provisions were already growing thin. Fifteen miles ahead the Colorado River carved its way through an unknown canyon. Four men were sent ahead to scout. They returned with a disheartening report. There was no way, they reported, that a wagon road could be built down to the Colorado. The party, to all intents and purposes, was trapped.

Today the Hole-in-the-Rock Trail, a fifty-five-mile-long dirt road, gives hikers and backpackers access to the many spectacular side-canyons that flow into the Escalante River from the south—Harris Wash, Scorpion Gulch, Willow Gulch, Dry Fork Coyote, Fortymile Gulch, Fiftymile Gulch, Davis Gulch, and the like. The whole wildly scenic region, declared the Grand Staircase–Escalante National Monument by President Bill Clinton in 1996, is thronged nowadays by recreationists. Yet on a dreary November day, forty miles out that dirt road, as the sleet and snow start to come down, you can easily recapture the sense of desolation that afflicted the Hole-in-the-Rock team as November 1879 slid into December.

Vaughn and I had both traveled the Hole-in-the-Rock trail and hiked some of those side-canyons; I had made some ten or twelve trips into that outback. On one of our trips, Vaughn and I stopped at Dance Hall Rock, an eerie hoodoo of dark red sandstone that erupts from the desert only a mile and a half northwest of Forty-Mile Spring.

Dance Hall Rock forms a natural amphitheater facing south with a surprisingly level floor. Here, in the midst of their winter-struck doldrums, the pilgrims several times buoyed their spirits by holding dances, with three fiddlers providing the music. Those defiant bouts of merrymaking may have started a tradition, for today the rock is covered with carved signatures and initials. On our own visit, Vaughn and I spent an hour at Dance Hall Rock perusing these old "Kilroys-were-here," finding several that dated from the Hole-in-the-Rock team.

By December 1879, the emigrants hoped to have reached Montezuma Creek. Instead, they had covered less than half their journey, with all the most serious obstacles ahead. The pilgrims had never dreamed that their "shortcut" would force them to pass the entire winter in the unforgiving wilderness. With retreat to Escalante cut off, they faced a potential ordeal akin to the one that had reduced the Donner Party to starvation and cannibalism thirty-three years earlier—and there were three times as many men, women, and children in the Hole-in-the-Rock expedition as there had been in the Donner entourage.

These Mormons, however, were made of much tougher stuff than the farmers from Illinois and Iowa who had come to grief at the foot of the Sierra Nevada. A second reconnaissance party made another trip to the cliff edge that overlooked the Colorado and discovered a natural cleft that they thought might just possibly—with a formidable effort to smooth and improve the route—serve as a "road" down to the great river. This cleft they named the Hole in the Rock.

It was, to be sure, a daunting prospect. Platte Lyman, one of the leaders of the party, wrote in his diary that "the walls of the Kanyon rise 2000 feet from the water and are in many places perpendicular." The top of the Hole is actually only a thousand feet above the river (the lower benches having since been inundated by Lake Powell), and the angle of the cleft at its steepest is about forty-five degrees, not vertical. Yet this gash in the bedrock was riddled with giant boulders, between which yawned deep holes. It was not obvious how to make a road here that could accommodate eighty-three wagons.

The decision was born of desperation. David E. Miller, the expedition historian, puts a doughty spin on the team's morale: "Gloom and despondency, which had pervaded the camp, were now replaced with optimism and good will. Road work that had come to a standstill with the return of the [initial] scouts was now recommenced. . . . There would be no more talk of turning back."

With the full party camped near the top of the cleft, work on the road commenced in mid-December. Picks, sledgehammers, shovels, crowbars, and chisels attacked the rock, aided by charges of blasting powder. Debris chopped and blasted loose from the upper part of the cleft was used as fill below. Yet it was not until January 25, 1880, that the workers declared the road ready for use.

The lowering of the eighty-three wagons was accomplished with ropes held by twenty men at a time, reinforced sometimes by horses or hitching posts planted in crevices along the path. Each wagon had two wheels locked with heavy chains to serve as brakes.

A few years ago, Vaughn and I hiked—scrambled, would be a better word—down the Hole in the Rock. Since 1880, the debris fill has eroded out, leaving the "road" much the same gauntlet of boulders and gaping pits that the pioneers must have first beheld. Even so, we were overwhelmed by the achievement of the Mormons, who got all their wagons down to the river without seriously damaging one. Then they floated the wagons across the current, while they rode and swam their horses and cattle.

Like Dance Hall Rock, the walls of Hole in the Rock, especially just below the rim, are festooned with incised signatures and initials. In another hour's close search, Vaughn and I found a number of graffiti that dated from the winter of 1879–80.

Once on the east side of the Colorado, the party was still far from the end of its tribulations. It took brilliant scouting by an advance team of four to find a way across Wilson Mesa, Grey Hills, Clay Hills, and especially Cedar Mesa, dissected by the fierce gorges of Grand Gulch, Slickhorn, Johns, Fish, Owl, and other canyons. Many a time over the years, Vaughn and I had driven or hiked pieces of the Hole-in-the-Rock Road, which still exists as a rutted trail across the northern end of Cedar Mesa.

Yet here, even the scouts began to fear they were lost. Only when those four explorers, in the middle of a snowstorm, topped out on a diminutive cone and caught sight of the Abajo Mountains ten miles away, which one of the scouts recognized from the earlier 1879 reconnaissance mission, did the team dare to believe it could complete its mission to Montezuma Creek. Salvation Knoll, as the grateful scouts named that hill, stands beside today's State Highway 95; a small plaque commemorates the breakthrough.

There would be one last barrier to the emigrants' shortcut—Comb Ridge. It was not until late March that the full party rolled their wagons down the Twist, a steep, switchbacking trail just north of Road Canyon, and gained the sandy, level draw of Comb Wash. But the ridge itself, looming sheer and unbroken above them to the east, looked uncrossable. The expedition trundled south down Comb Wash. They discovered the Navajo horse trail across the Comb, the same route that would later be dynamited into Highway 163, but could see no way to get wagons up it. Pushing on, they clung to a single hope—that they could round the Comb on the south, right on the banks of the San Juan, and forge a road through to Montezuma Creek along the north shore of that river.

Alas, the cliffs that plunged to the river for miles east of the Comb precluded any hope of a road. So the exhausted pioneers turned to the Comb itself. Up what they would name San Juan Hill, by the very route that Vaughn, Greg, and I hiked on September 12, they painstakingly crafted another zigzagging wagon-way. Writes Miller, "San Juan Hill proved almost too much for the worn-out teams, weakened by a long winter of hard work without sufficient feed."

Charles Redd, son of one of the four advance scouts, left a vivid description of the terrible labor of pulling the wagons up that steep, stony, 500-foot rise:

> *Here again seven span of horses were used, so that when some of the horses were on their knees, fighting to get up to find a foothold, the still-erect horses could plunge upward against the sharp grade. On the worst slopes the men were forced to beat their jaded animals into giving all they had. After several pulls, rests, and pulls, many of the horses took to spasms and near convulsions, so exhausted were they. By the time most of the outfits were across, the worst stretches could easily be identified by the dried blood and matted hair from the forelegs of the struggling teams.*

By April 6—nearly six months after the party had set out from Cedar City—the played-out pilgrims were camped on the site of today's town of Bluff. Rather than push on the mere fifteen miles to Montezuma Creek, they decided to build their stronghold against the Gentiles here. Writes Miller, "All at once the energy seems to have left them completely. The travel-worn expedition was just too tired to go on." Astonishingly, the team had lost not a single member but instead gained two, who were born along the way.

For the casual visitor today, Bluff seems a far more appealing place to build a town—nestled as it is between handsome facing sandstone cliffs, with acre upon acre of fertile river bottom—than Montezuma Creek, a wind-blown hamlet occupied now almost entirely by Navajos. Scattered around the orderly grid of Bluff's streets stand a number of houses built by the Hole-in-the-Rock pioneers, among them Jens Nielson, Willard Butt, Kumen Jones, and Hyrum Perkins. Those houses, sturdily constructed in the Mormon style with big, shaped chunks of brown stone, have withstood the ravages of time. A few still sport the twin balconies with separate staircases by which the patriarchs made their nightly choices among their plural wives as discreetly as possible.

Yet a final irony serves as an epitaph to the heroic Hole-in-the-Rock expedition. The pioneers found Bluff a difficult place to maintain. Indian depredations kept the residents on their toes, and recurrent floods, as the San Juan overflowed its banks, reaching from cliff to cliff, wiped out years of efforts to build dams and irrigation ditches and to plant fields. Within only thirty years after establishing their bastion against the Gentiles in southeast Utah, most of the families, turning their backs on farming in favor of ranching as a way of life, had moved north to found the towns of Blanding and Monticello, which remain solidly Mormon today. Meanwhile Bluff, its three hundred residents now comprising rafters, llama outfitters, artists, writers, archaeologists, and guides such as Vaughn, likes to boast that it is the least-Mormon town in Utah.

———— ∞∞∞ ————

Climbing San Juan Hill and sweating profusely in the ninety-degree heat, the three of us saw no dried blood or matted hair to testify to the Saints' long-ago passage, but we were delighted to find, along a stretch that exceeded a mile in length, specimens of the expert crib-work with which they had shored up their road, as well as to see the faint ruts left by their wagon wheels still creasing the hard ground. In no rush once we reached the crest of the Comb, we strolled along, treating ourselves to two rest stops, one for lunch and one so that Greg could dry out his feet (he had worn his boots on the San Juan ford, while Vaughn and I had donned our sandals).

Two miles north of the San Juan, we overlooked a prosperous-looking assemblage of buildings on the bench above Butler Wash, only 250 feet below us to the east. Vaughn knew the camp as the homestead of the Black family, Navajo friends of many of the folks in Bluff. Virginia Black was an expert weaver, whom Vaughn and Marcia had commissioned to make a table runner for their home. "Virginia would come over," Vaughn amplified now, as we looked down on the camp, "to have Marcia read her letters from her clients and write responses"—because her English was imperfect.

Within the last year, Vaughn and Jim Hook, both of whom served as volunteer fire fighters, called out on many a rescue as well as to douse conflagrations, had gotten a call that there had been a bad car accident on Route 191, which heads south from Bluff to Mexican Water. They were among the first on the scene, where, to their horror, they discovered Virginia Black dead in a head-on collision with a pickup that had crossed the center line. During the previous decade or so, that harmless-seeming stretch of highway, with few bends and no cliffs shelving from its margins, had seen far more than its share of fatal accidents, almost as though it formed one of those places the Diné knew to shun as harboring some capacity for evil imprinted into the very landscape.

By 4:00 PM, we stood at the top of the artificial cliff blasted through the Comb by Highway 163. Below us stretched the black asphalt ribbon, its yellow center line proscribing passing on the dangerous curve that lay just to the west. The sight came as a shock. As we hovered, a car or two whizzed through the gap—alien machines invading our solitude. I found myself thinking, *Do cars really go that fast?*

We scuttled down, looked both ways, and strode across the asphalt, the strangest surface our boots had trod in twelve days. A few hundred yards to the east, we branched off on an old dirt road that angled north to the disused former highway—older lumps of grayer asphalt crumbling in the pitiless sun, weeds growing through their cracks. For our campsite, Vaughn had his mind set on a little alcove just up ahead that he had visited several times before. We reached it in half an hour. Pulling out our sat phone, I dialed up Marcia to give her directions to the resupply spot.

It would have been absurd not to camp here, near the highway. Accordingly, we had planned the evening of September 12 not only as a resupply, but as a reunion and a picnic. Yet in retrospect, all three of us would wonder whether that soirée just off the asphalt had been a mistake.

The snug alcove facing southeast was evidently a townie party hangout. Broken glass littered the floor of the small wash, and the back wall had been spray-painted with the deathless motto, "I LOVE YOU KC ALWAYS." Next to this graffito was a painted portrait of a marijuana plant—which, to Vaughn and Greg's vast amusement, I didn't recognize as such. Yet old layers of soot coating the ceiling of the deepest recesses of the alcove proved that the Anasazi had had their own parties here long before the townies arrived.

Rather than having us cook up another freeze-dried beef stew or turkey and mashed potatoes, Marcia had stopped at the K&C convenience store in Bluff to pick up several gas-station pizzas. She had also brought more beer from Vaughn's larder—both Tecate and Moosehead. The dinner was a welcome change from glop, but the K&C pizzas, though unquestionably the best (the only?) available in Bluff, were nothing to write home about. Afterward, I felt stuffed to the bursting point—"pogged," in the Aussie slang Greg had introduced to our trip. And the woozy buzz that suffused me after three or four Tecates had little of the transport about it that the single can I had guzzled that morning had imparted. It was depressing how quickly and routinely, after nearly two weeks of abstinence, the sorrows of gin (in this case, of good Mexican beer) could reassert their numbing hold.

Despite his protestations in recent days—"The kid'll be fine without me for a couple of weeks"—Greg was unabashedly happy to see Ariann. He held the baby in his arms for half an hour at a time, cooing nonsense syllables. He even changed a diaper.

Having to get up early the next morning to go to work in Blanding, where she served as assistant to the curator of the Edge of the Cedars Museum, Marcia left our campout after dinner. Renée and Ariann, however, spent the night. I dug my two-man tent out of a resupply duffel to serve as their bedroom. Just before going to sleep, I visited the trio. In the light of my headlamp, their ménage formed a tableau out of Norman Rockwell: Greg and Renée in their bags on either side of Ariann, bundled up in piles of fleece and down.

The Comb Gets Rough

Lying on the full-length, leakless Therm-a-Rest I had seized from the resupply, I slept well that night, despite being subliminally aware of the sound of trucks and cars on Highway 163, even in the wee hours. Not Greg. The baby, so contented during the picnic, sleeping off the long drive from Castle Valley, became an insomniac. She stirred, thrashed, and whimpered for hours. Knowing how badly Greg needed to sleep, Renée tried to shush her, but Ariann was not taking well to her first night of camping out.

In the morning, Greg looked flat-out wasted. He swore that he had gotten at most five minutes of sleep. In addition, the pizza and beer had roiled up a hiatal hernia that had plagued him throughout the previous year.

We were off at 8:30 AM. The heat wave had not begun to break: by mid-morning, we guessed, the temperature was up to ninety degrees. With four days' food and some seven quarts of water apiece, our packs again weighed at least sixty-five pounds each. Greg lagged in the rear all day, emitting grotesque, rasping belches, a couple of times leaning over his knees as he tried unsuccessfully to throw up. Stupidly, I asked him how he felt. "I'm sick as fuck, that's how," he answered. When we took rest breaks, Greg sprawled face-up on the bedrock like an invalid carried in by stretcher from the battlefield.

The malaise that hung over our morning, however, was as much spiritual as digestive. The amenities of our campout—drive-in pizza and beer, reunion with loved ones, spray-painted graffiti, and the rumble of eighteen-wheelers gearing up for the pass through the Comb—had the effect of momentarily trivializing our trip. After twelve days of the most splendid isolation, broken only by Jim Hook's brief and efficient resupplies and by the cryptic encounter with the old sheepherder, Maxie Platt, we had been plunged back into the hectic ordinariness of our quotidian lives. We needed a stiff few days of backpacking to rejuvenate the mission of our traverse.

But naturally, September 13 would prove to be our hardest day of all on the Comb Ridge. Here one sandstone tooth after another soared out of the low notches on either side. Trying to stay near the crest, we made several routefinding mistakes, having to backtrack in the face of cliffs that suddenly plunged from beneath our boots. The slabs across which we strode were constantly tilted from upper left to lower right, straining our ankles. I had to concentrate hard not to stumble and fall. The heat was unrelenting, and despite the great shape we were in, our packs felt like "pigs" again. I later estimated that in eight hours of fairly steady hiking, we gained only nine miles, though I thought that if we had some way to measure the vagaries of the path we actually followed step-by-step, we could add half again that distance to our day's plod. "Up and down, up and down," I wrote that evening in my journal. "Monotonous and grueling." I estimated also that we must have gained and lost a full 2000 feet of altitude as we wound along the rugged crest—by far the most of any day yet.

The ordeal seemed to bring out Vaughn's latent machismo. "This is fun," he asserted, in response to one of my groans upon beholding yet another plunging notch ahead. And he seemed to take for granted that Greg would hobble along, no matter how much discomfort he was in.

To be sure, Vaughn lived by the code he silently espoused. Many a time, I had seen him hike all day with some painful ailment—his plantar fasciitis, within the previous year—about which he uttered not a word of complaint. In Vaughn's book, you sucked it up and got ahead with it, whether "it" was fiscal woes or impossibly demanding clients or the grim trudge yawning between here and camp. And that day, Greg sucked it up with the best of them. His performance in covering those nine (or fifteen) miles of ceaseless up and down, sleepless and "sick as fuck," was one of the gutsiest I had ever seen in the backcountry. (No wonder, I thought, he had survived so many all-out campaigns in the Himalaya.)

The heat and exertion were taking their toll on all three of us, even Vaughn. By mid-afternoon, we all had hot spots on the soles of our feet, the first threat of new blisters in more than a week. To add to his miseries, Greg's pinched toes had rubbed raw in his sweaty boots.

Around 3:00 PM, as I scrambled up yet another nasty barrier of talus and broken cliffs, I suddenly burst out, "I hate the Comb!" Vaughn laughed out loud. Even Greg uttered a guffaw.

Adding to my weariness with the day's march was the fact that we found almost no signs of the ancients among all these prongs and cols. The significant exception was a trench of upright slabs in the sand that Vaughn discovered. He thought it was a kiln, a place where the Anasazi had fired their pots. Oddly, such kilns have proved among the most elusive of structures left by the Old Ones.

With respect to the Anasazi, there was a kind of catch-22 built into our traverse. We all felt honor-bound to stay near the crest as much as we could. Vaughn in particular was keen to stick to the high road. On those sections where we had skirted the crest on the east or west (as on the two-and-a-half-mile shortcut from one bend of the Chinle to another on September 9), we felt as though we were cheating. Yet as we had known even before launching the trip, the preponderance of ruins and rock art appeared lower on the east slope of the Comb. Were we to maximize our chances of finding signs of the ancients, we would strike out low on those eastern skirts, poking up each side-canyon as we came to it. Throughout the journey, we would find not a single substantial ruin on or near the crest, and precious little rock art.

North of the San Juan, we had laid no water caches. That decision was predicated on Vaughn's conviction that in the stretch of Comb he knew best, from years of guiding, he could always find water pockets in even the driest of times. Not coincidentally, however—for those same potholes and tanks had slaked the thirst of the Old Ones—the best place to look for water was also low on the east slope, in the dark bends of defiles where the sun seldom penetrated.

But it had now been nine days since the last true rainstorm. I was a bit alarmed that, after six hours of hiking on September 13, we had found not a single pothole holding even a cupful of life-giving water. Finally, I stumbled across a diminutive pool. Convinced there would be more of the same, we passed it by without filling up. Yet when another half-hour's hike revealed no further pools, Vaughn said, "When we come to a water hole like that one, we should pump and just slam down a quart." I agreed.

At last, around 4:00 pm, following Vaughn's lead, we headed off the crest, down to the east to look for a campsite with water. And now ensued another spat between Vaughn and me, born of the day's frustrations. Low in a scrubby side-canyon, we came to a stagnant-looking though eminently potable tank in the weeds. I suggested pumping a quart or two, but Vaughn, in mute answer, simply marched on. He was carrying our pump, so I shrugged my shoulders and followed him.

We came to another small tank, the water noticeably clearer than that in the previous hole. I stopped and said, "Let's pump."

Vaughn shot back, "I've got three quarts. I'm fine. You can pump if you want to."

Finally he surrendered the pump. Greg and I filled a couple of bottles, as I nursed my annoyance. It had done no good to point out that I was simply repeating Vaughn's own advice to stop and "slam down a quart." By the time Greg and I got our packs back on, Vaughn was out of sight ahead. Later I would write in my journal, "What is this macho trip he's on? He is in the best shape of the three of us, but I've never seen him like this." Later Vaughn insisted, "I was sure we weren't far from better water. And as it turned out, we weren't."

Yet as afternoon slid toward evening, an amicable mood settled over our threesome. At last we had found a good campsite, so low it was near the very base of the Comb, but on a level bench on which we could spread out our tents where we pleased, beside two generous pools of water. (Why did these potholes, exposed to the blazing sun, retain the rainfall of September 4, while so many other tanks higher on the ridge had dried up? Here was one of the conundrums of the Comb that we would never solve.)

A crescent new moon now hung in the west, just above the distant crest of the ridge. I cooked up a dinner of freeze-dried chili enlivened with cornbread crackers and squirt-tubes of cheese. It was actually a relief not to be tempted by beer. The only drawback about our camp was that the worst hordes of mosquitoes we had yet seen hovered in the still air. "Something's all screwed up," said Vaughn, batting away a cloud of bugs, "maybe because of the drought." For the last seven years, most of the Southwest had been afflicted by annual precipitation totals far below normal. By the summer of 2004, Lake Powell had shrunk to its lowest level since the reservoir had filled in the late 1950s. Yet it seemed counterintuitive that drought might produce mosquitoes—the prevailing wisdom being that wetness breeds the noxious whining insects, as in Alaska, where in summer the permafrost melts and turns the tundra into wall-to-wall bog.

Both Greg and I slept well that night, though Greg still looked groggy in the morning. It was Vaughn's turn to endure a bad night, as he discovered that his Therm-a-Rest half-pad had sprung an alarmingly fast leak. The only way to repair a Therm-a-Rest in the field is to blow it up and submerge it in water to locate the column of bubbles that betrays the leak. Now, in the morning, Vaughn plunged his pad into one of our drinking pools and found the telltale pin-sized hole. "Cactus spine," he muttered as he applied a patch.

We were approaching the central stretch of the Comb between the twin highways bisecting the ridge west of Bluff and Blanding. This was the terrain that Vaughn knew best, for it was the richest in ruins and rock art along that whole twenty-mile expanse. The first of our mandatory visits would be to the Procession Panel, located on the west wall of an obscure lump of billowing stone only a few hundred yards below the crest of the Comb. I had seen the panel three or four times before, Vaughn at least a dozen times; but Greg had never been there.

In only forty minutes on the morning of September 14, we traversed the apron of the Comb and reached the draw that led up to the Procession Panel. Despite my three or four prior visits, I still had trouble recognizing that draw, but along this part of the Comb, Vaughn pretty much had the approaches "wired." It was here that his method of orienting in the canyon country demonstrated one of its advantages over mine. I relied heavily on the topo maps, which I took pride in being able to read skillfully. Vaughn seldom carried a map, relying instead on a head full of memorized landmarks. The problem with the current topo map, the Bluff SW quadrangle, was that every one of a dozen short but deeply grooved defiles leading from the foot of the Comb to its crest looked the same, a mile-long in-curve in the brown contour lines that modeled the crests and creases of this geological prodigy.

Dropping our backpacks, we carried only a quart or two of water apiece along the beaten trail that angled up the side-canyon. After the previous day's marathon trudge, this unencumbered detour was sheer delight. By 9:20, we were face-to-face with the single most extraordinary

The masterpiece of Procession Panel, with its parade of figures marching to a central point

rock art panel on the whole Comb Ridge—one of the finest panels, for that matter, in all the Southwest. And though by now its details were familiar to me, I felt all over again a shiver of awe at beholding this prehistoric masterpiece. Greg, with his camera, was beside himself.

⬿⬿⬿

The story of the discovery of Procession Panel—or the rediscovery, for surely certain Anglos must have blundered across the site in earlier decades—is a fascinating one. By the late 1980s, day hikers had begun to throng this section of the Comb, and its more famous sites, such as Fishmouth and Monarch Caves, were visited every week. But at that time, no one (as far as Vaughn or I could ascertain) knew about this peerless petroglyph panel.

Winston Hurst, Vaughn's and my archaeologist friend, who had grown up in Blanding, had told me that one day near the end of the 1980s, as he helped his artist friend Joe Pachak paint rock art reproductions on the walls of the Edge of the Cedars Museum (of which Winston then served as curator), a stranger approached, described the Procession Panel, and asked if Winston or Joe knew of the site. The fellow, as Winston recalled, was a schoolteacher from Kayenta. Winston passed on the information to his friend and fellow devotee of things Anasazi, Owen Severance. Electrified, Severance took off at once up the proper side-canyon, found the panel, and photographed it.

"Owen walked into the museum with his slides," Winston recalled. "I thought, how cool is this? And then, as we held the slides in our hands, a guy and his kid walked in. The guy said that ten or fifteen years ago, he had found an amazing rock art site, but he couldn't find it again. He then described the Procession Panel. 'Is this it?' I asked, showing him the slides. 'Yeah, that's it,' he said.

"It's like in just a two- or three-week period, somebody had thrown a switch. And within a year, there was a beaten path up to the Procession Panel."

The "procession" that gives the panel its name is a tight column of human figures marching from right to left across a rock canvas that stretches an astounding twenty-eight yards from end to end. These petroglyphs range from one and a half to five inches tall. Counting the figures, as I had on each visit, I numbered 154 humanoids. Taken all together, they suggest some pilgrimage toward a mystical but preordained goal; yet among their details is an entrancing variety of specificities. Some of the marchers are adumbrated with the most cursory of swipes, as abstract and yet suggestive as Matisse paper cut-outs. Others have incised legs, as finely carved as if they had been cut with a pen-knife, sprouting from blob-like torsos. One pilgrim, taller than his neighbors, carries a crooked staff and has a duck sitting on his head. Six marchers seem to be stomping across the recumbent body of a much larger humanoid felled face-up in the path. Five other marchers are turned to face the viewer, right arms raised in greeting. Two others are dueling with atlatls. The whole procession is molded in three dimensions to fit the idiosyncrasies of the natural surface: at one point on the right end of the panel, the marchers emerge from a crack and turn a sharp protruding corner without missing a step.

Counterpointing the procession is a group of bighorn sheep, much larger than the human figures, going against the flow as they move from left to right. Most of the sheep have been ritually re-pecked, with swaths of lighter patina gouged across such vital parts as head, neck, heart, genitals, and leg joints. Unlike the defaced panels we had seen on our second day on the Comb, these re-peckings were most likely the work of later Anasazi, not of Navajos. (The panel is unmistakably from the Basketmaker era.) Some rock art experts argue that such retouching signifies not the destruction of illness-producing images (as seems to be the case with the Navajo deface-ments), but the effort to reanimate the animals as sympathetic magic ensuring a bountiful hunt.

Two very large deer stand near the center of the panel. One has an atlatl dart protruding from its underbelly; the other boasts a long tail that metamorphoses at its end into a snake with jaws open, ready to strike.

Now Vaughn pointed at an enigmatic design and said, "I'll bet that's a trophy head." Anasazi pictographs and petroglyphs found elsewhere in the Southwest seem to show humans holding decapi-tated heads with handles affixed atop the crowns, and a small num-ber of such grisly "trophies"—heads removed from bodies, the skull separated from the flesh and discarded, the face sometimes painted in broad bands, with carrying handles attached—have been found ar-chaeologically. The notion behind a trophy head is that some warrior, having slain an enemy, turned the decapitated, boneless head into a totem to carry into further battle, either as sympathetic war magic or simply to terrify his opponents. (So much for the "little people of peace," as sentimentalists throughout the twentieth century liked to characterize the Hopi and their ancestors!)

No rock art tableau that I had seen anywhere in the world tantalized me more than the Procession Panel. After counting the marching figures, I simply stared, as I lapsed into a trance, begging the unfathomable meaning of the whole composition to slip into my subconscious. On the basis of style, all three of us agreed that the whole panel was most likely the work of a single artist, a Michelangelo of the first millennium before Christ, perhaps, whose name and identity would remain forever lost.

Three years before, Vaughn and I, on separate outings, had hiked up to the Procession Panel to be stunned by a geological cataclysm. Sometime within the previous several months, a huge section of the cliff had collapsed. The debris, ranging from jagged boulders to fine dust, lay sprawled across the ground like the wreckage of some dynamited roadcut. The left-hand edge of the collapsed cliff lay only three yards from the right-hand edge of the panel.

As we descended the beaten path and came in sight of our backpacks, a pair of men appeared below us on the trail, heading upward. Vaughn and Greg passed them with a perfunctory greeting, but I stopped to chat. The two were a burly man in his late forties or fifties and a younger fellow, perhaps the other man's son. The older guy did all the talking. They were from Crestone, Colorado, a tiny burg nestled under the Sangre de Cristo Range on the east edge of the San Luis Valley.

"You're the first other hikers we've seen in fourteen days," I said. "We've come all the way from Kayenta—almost a hundred miles."

I expected some reaction, or at least a question or two about our outlandish journey, but the burly man did not even grunt in acknowledgment, while his "son" stared at the ground, as if impatient to resume the hike.

"Is the Butler Wash road open?" I asked. Surprised during the last day and a half not to see a single vehicle on that usually busy thoroughfare east of the Comb, we had begun to wonder whether the September 4 storm had washed it out.

"The Butler road's always open," the heavyset man answered condescendingly. "Where're you from?"

"I grew up in Colorado," I answered, "but I live in Boston."

"I feel sorry for you."

Well, fuck you, buddy, I thought as I headed on down the path to catch up with Greg and Vaughn. I recounted the exchange.

"Yeah, I run into that kind of thing all the time out here," said Vaughn. Come to think of it, so had I. All across the Southwest, when strangers meet on the trail and stop to talk, a kind of one-upmanship often suffuses the dialogue. "You been up the left fork?" one may say to the other. "Yeah, but only as far as that big ruin." "You oughta keep going. There's great stuff all the way to the headwaters." Each party is determined, in a few phrases, to establish his credentials as a true connoisseur of the backcountry, so instead of a sincere exchange of information, a kind of contest takes over—topographical name-dropping disguised as hail-fellow-well-met.

On Cedar Mesa, in fact, just two years before, I had been goaded into a rage by a woman I had run into at a ruin I had visited many times before. She, her companion, and her dog had been eating lunch when I arrived. I could feel her censorious eyes watching my every move as I poked through the masoned dwellings, sticking my head inside a couple of windows. When my hand lightly brushed the wall next to one window, I was not entirely surprised to hear her clear her throat, then recite in an unctuous voice, "We're members of a group called Friends of Cedar Mesa, and we believe you shouldn't touch the cliff dwellings."

"I don't need you to tell me how to visit a ruin," I shot back.

An uneasy silence ensued. "Isn't that a nice-looking kiva?" the woman gushed.

"It's not a kiva," I answered, barely suppressing an appended, "you idiot."

The pair gathered up their picnic and started to leave. As she headed out, the Friend of Cedar Mesa couldn't resist saying, "It's just that human skin has these oils on it, and that can deface—"

"Yeah, yeah," I cut her off. "How about eating lunch in a ruin? How about taking dogs into ruins?"

"Have a nice day," she sang out, her back turned as she hiked away. It took me two hours to regain my equanimity. But then I thought, what was my problem? Why did I have to prove to the sanctimonious scold that I knew more about ruins than she did? Why couldn't I let her pious strictures roll harmlessly off my back?

Now, backpacking north, we stayed low on the slopes of the Comb, for our next stop would be Monarch Cave, approachable only from the east. Once more, Vaughn was in his charging mode, leading at a pace I could barely keep up with. Greg fell farther and farther behind, so I took upon myself a role that I had come to resent during the previous two weeks—that of middle man keeping an equidistance between leader and straggler, striving to stay in sight of both.

At 11:30, Vaughn scrambled down into the draw that both of us recognized as the one that led to Monarch. I joined him in the shade of a cottonwood, where we threw off our packs and sat down to wait for Greg. I kept an eye out, however, for I knew that Greg had never been to Monarch and thus would not recognize the correct draw.

Sure enough, I glimpsed Greg as he struck the draw thirty yards east of us, never saw us in our cottonwood nook, scrambled up the far bank, and headed on into the north. I jogged after him, scuttling up to the rim, and then called out his name to rein him in. Greg turned, puzzled, and rejoined me without a word.

When we got back to Vaughn, I couldn't resist an I-told-you-so. "See, that's what I was afraid might happen," I griped.

Vaughn shrugged. "We'd have found him."

"But what's the point? It would just be a big waste of time."

Vaughn didn't answer, but now, as he led the way up the side-canyon, he moderated his pace. "Too bad," I wrote later in my journal, describing the contretemps—"the central tension of the trip. But Greg lets it slide, as I can't."

Monarch Cave forms a huge alcove where an otherwise nondescript side-canyon suddenly boxes out. The pouroff at the upper lip of the overhang channels a minor waterfall every time it rains, and in consequence, the hollow at the foot of the fall has formed one of the most reliable tanks for miles around. That deep pothole, sunk low beneath the north-facing cliff that constricts the canyon, in the shade most of the day even in midsummer, would in fact prove to hold the single largest volume of water we would find on the whole traverse.

For the Anasazi, Monarch Cave must have been a near-paradise. The two-story, free-standing cliff dwelling they built inside the spacious alcove must, in its pristine state, have been the most lordly of all the Pueblo III villages erected along this stretch of Comb Ridge. Even in its present-day dilapidation, the ruin retains a haunting grandeur. But Monarch is one of those sites that, in the canyon-lover's jargon, has been truly "hammered." On my previous visits, I had more often than not had to share the cave with other enthusiasts who had made the easy half-hour hike in from a pullout on the Butler Wash

The fortress-like towers of Monarch Cave

road. Once I had watched a teenager, scrambling up to the ruin from the more difficult southern approach, as he grabbed the base of a room wall to pull himself up and dislodged a mortared stone that clattered and then fell into the tank below. The bumbler did not even seem to realize that he had committed a faux pas. Other times I had watched as visitors trod obliviously on top of bedrock petroglyphs along the more normal northern approach.

At Monarch, I had always found it hard to separate my dismay at the disturbance wrought by the hundreds (thousands?) of visitors every year from my appreciation of what a remarkable ruin it was, despite those ravages. Even well-meaning passersby had performed their mischief. It was hard to find a single potsherd lying in the dirt outside the cave, but several boulders behind the ruin were covered with sherds that had been picked up elsewhere and left there in ostentatious display. Archaeologists, who call these collections "museum rocks" or "goody piles," rue the loss of the sherds' provenience those assemblages portend. Often over the years, I had watched as Vaughn strode up to a goody pile and angrily swept it from the boulder, scattering the sherds in the surrounding dirt. He had since had a change of heart, however, having observed firsthand that wrecking a goody pile only encouraged subsequent visitors to build bigger and better ones. At heavily visited sites, it was perhaps the lesser of two evils to leave the damn collections in place.

Now, in Monarch Cave, I noticed that, despite the show of magnanimity implied by leaving the sherds for others to enjoy, there were only gray pieces of pottery in these goody piles. All the prettier polychrome sherds—which we had come across in such prodigal abundance along the Comb on the Navajo Reservation—had long since disappeared into the pockets of souvenir hunters, many of whom had probably said to themselves, *I'll just keep one. Nobody will miss just one sherd.*

Likewise, several scalloped depressions on the boulders' upper surfaces—sharpening grooves, archaeologists call them, inferring that they may have been worn by Anasazi honing their chert tools and weapons—were filled now with desiccated corncobs, another well-meaning misinterpretation on the part of visitors who mistook the depressions for bedrock metates used to grind corn.

Other signs left by twentieth-century tourists could hardly be construed as well-meaning, including a collection of inscriptions and signatures scraped with knives or scrawled with burnt sticks on the back wall of the cave. One of these annotations read "TIMS WHORE HOUSE." Yet amidst the graffiti, a neatly chiseled inscription stood out:

I. A. E. Exped.
MONARCH'S CAVE
1892.

Therein, we knew, hung an interesting tale.

———∞∞∞———

By the early 1890s, curiosity about the prehistoric ruins found so well-preserved all across the Southwest had spurred a number of ambitious expeditions in the field. For the most part, these were undertaken by ranchers living near the Four Corners, particularly in southwestern Colorado. Preeminent among these amateur devotees were the Wetherills of Mancos: Richard, John, and their brothers Al, Clayton, and Winslow. On a winter day in 1888, out chasing stray cows on Mesa Verde in a snowstorm, Richard and his brother-in-law Charlie Mason stumbled upon Cliff Palace, the largest cliff dwelling in the United States. Within the next few years, the Wetherills were digging extensively in Cliff Palace and other nearby ruins.

These ranchers soon discovered that there was a market for their booty. Some of the rich assemblages of artifacts, skeletons, and mummies they hauled out of the ruins found their way to museums, mostly in the East; others vanished into the black holes of private collections.

The Wetherills had keen competition, particularly in the persons of two Durango ranchers, Charles McLoyd and Charles Cary Graham. By today's standards, the excavations those cowboys carried out look like the most brutal kind of pothunting and grave-robbing, but in 1890 there was no established standard for such work. It was not yet illegal to dig up Indian ruins on public lands (the Antiquities Act would not be passed until 1906, in large measure as a response to Richard Wetherill's excavations at Chaco Canyon). Some of these early diggers were indeed little better than vandals, and the loss to science of the understanding of the great ruins they wrecked by excavating them remains an imperishable tragedy. Others, however—most notably, Richard Wetherill—taught themselves to record the sites they dug and the artifacts they recovered in great detail. Though it would take a century to rehabilitate his reputation, Richard Wetherill is today viewed by most experts as at least as good an archaeologist as many a professional who followed him into the field.

By 1892, however, not one academically trained archaeologist had dug in the Southwest. A new demand for relics from the cliff dwellings had arisen, in the form of the upcoming World's Columbian Exposition, to be held in Chicago in 1893. Out of this ferment was born the Illustrated American Exploring Expedition.

The leader of the party was Warren K. Moorehead, a twenty-six-year-old Ohioan with university training who had dug in the prehistoric mounds at Hopewell and Adena. Most of the rest of the party of seven, comprising an art instructor, a surveyor, an entomologist, and a natural scientist, among others, were also from Ohio. The expedition had influential backers. It was jointly sponsored by the Smithsonian Institution, the American Museum of Natural History, and Harvard's Peabody Museum. Among the benefactors were two railroad companies that offered free passage from New York City to Durango; two biscuit companies that provided much of the food; Colgate, which supplied soap; and both Winchester and Colt, the two leading American makers of firearms of the day. The principal sponsor was *Illustrated American* magazine, a weekly journal published in New York City, for which Moorehead and his lieutenant, Lewis W. Gunkel, would furnish regular reports from the field, under the rubric "In Search of a Lost Race."

It did not take long after reaching Durango, however, for these midwestern tenderfeet to realize they had bitten off more than they could chew. Traveling on an ambitious zigzagging loop down the Animas and La Plata Rivers to the San Juan, down that river to the mouth of McElmo Creek, and up McElmo, where they made the first report of the striking free-standing Anasazi towers of Hovenweep, now a national monument, the team struggled with the grueling logistics of desert travel. After nearly breaking down on the sandy wagon road to Bluff, Moorehead lamented in the *Illustrated American*, "For my part, I would rather walk five miles on an Ohio pike than one mile on any of the 'roads' in Southern Utah."

Though the correspondents strived to keep up their enthusiasm as they described the discovery and excavation of one Anasazi ruin after another, the whole team was plainly more appalled than delighted by the desert Southwest. In plain language, the Ohioans were homesick. Toward the end of the trip Moorehead confessed in print, "You cast your eyes about you to see something of beauty, but you see nothing save great frowning sandstone cliffs, an occasional crow, a coyote, or a sand crane. You sigh for the green fields and shady woods of the East." At camp each night, "everyone comes in tired and hungry. The main desire on the part of everyone is to get through as rapidly as possible and return to the delights of the East."

In this demoralized state, the team of seven set out on one last exploring jag from Bluff up Butler Wash. In early May, stumbling up yet another small side-canyon in the Comb Ridge, they discovered and named Monarch Cave—"for it must have been," wrote Gunkel, "the monarch of all it surveyed." Ranchers had no doubt found the alcove with the massive cliff dwelling before 1892, but the *Illustrated American* issue of August 6, 1892, marks its first appearance in print.

The party seems to have genuinely relished the beauty of this dead-end canyon with its impressive ruin. "Here," wrote Gunkel, "instead of stunted sage-brush, we find a luxurious growth of large, wide-spreading cottonwood trees, giving delightful shade from the hot sun; and beautiful shrubbery and flowering plants, and cool running water." Why, Monarch Cave was almost as good as Ohio!

In the pages of the magazine, Gunkel laid out a precise description of the ruin, complete with a floor-plan sketch. The team emphasized the defensive character of the cliff dwelling: "In one room alone we counted twenty-five portholes. From these the defenders could send their deadly arrows in every direction, up or down the canyon. . . . The entire aspect of the cave is of defense and protection, rather than comfort." Today's experts doubt that the "portholes" served as shafts through which to shoot arrows, but in 2004, the three of us could still peer through many of the loopholes—tubes for spying on intruders, most likely—that Moorehead and Co. had discovered 112 years before.

The team chiseled the record of its visit on the back wall and dug several rooms, hauling out "a few neatly worked stone axes and arrow heads, pieces of matting, short sticks with balls of pitch on the end for torches, pieces of string, and many corncobs and husks." Some of these artifacts were exhibited the next year at the Columbian Exposition. Where they rest today is probably an insoluble question.

So the "hammering" of Monarch Cave began as early as 1892, with its Anglo discoverers. Yet throughout their journey, Moorehead and Gunkel complain about signs of previous vandalism in the sites they visit. They even feel that in a sense they have come too late. "Cowboys and Indians," Moorehead gripes in the August 20 *Illustrated American*, "tempted by the flattering offers made them by traders, have despoiled the ruins and the relics easiest of access."

Indians? In 1892 most Navajos would not have gone near an Anasazi ruin, let alone looted it. But perhaps Moorehead was right. The Utes, who roamed Butler Wash as frequently as the Navajos, did not share their Athapaskan neighbors' terror of the places of the dead. And in the starvation economy of the 1890s, the promise of money might have bent even the Diné's deep-seated taboos. In *Sacred Land, Sacred View*, Robert McPherson records a dolorous early-twentieth-century echo of that pillage: "A man in Shonto reported that after extended windstorms in the spring or intense cloudbursts in the summer Navajo shepherds brought into the nearby trading post pots, ladles, and bowls exposed by the storms. In exchange, the seller received five cents' worth of hard candy in a brown paper sack."

On September 14, Greg, Vaughn, and I spent a good two hours in Monarch Cave. No other visitors wandered up the side-canyon while we were there. I turned my attention to the rich but subtle congeries of pictographs and petroglyphs that spread in a crescendoing array toward the ruin as you walk into it from the right-hand side. In my journal I noted "white and green triangles, red handprints, sharpening grooves. On the ceiling itself, big semi-abstract designs. . . . Green skeletal handprints (very faint). All kinds of bedrock stuff—mortars, petroglyphs, steps. . . . White handprints, some negative. Beam sockets. 'Practice' baby Moqui steps. Yellow handprints."

Greg turned a blind lens to the graffiti and goody piles as he scrambled all over the box canyon, trying to frame Monarch's felicities in his camera. Vaughn, who had been here more times than he could count, lay on his back and took a short nap.

Just outside the ruin, the BLM had installed an ammo box painted red and chained to a tree. Vaughn and I had come across these boxes in other heavily visited ruins, mostly on Cedar Mesa. The intentions of the agency were admirable, for the ammo box contained sheets printed with beginners' lessons in matters Anasazi, as well as "thou-shalt-nots" for visiting fragile ruins. Yet Vaughn and I agreed that the presence of these boxes—especially with their screaming red paint—was obnoxious, one more symptom of how the site had been hammered.

The box also contained a register in which visitors were encouraged to record their thoughts. I had always found these logs priceless repositories of the banal, full of platitudes scribbled down in response to what, for all I knew, had been genuine awe. I started reading entries out loud. From a Hugo, Oklahoma, couple: "Our 2nd trip back. I *love* the children's handprints." Children? The Anasazi had smaller hands than we do. Another: "Great—thanks for letting us come here." You'd think the BLM had built Monarch Cave as a theme park. A self-styled Thoreau or Ed Abbey: "Just me, a canyon wren, and 8 million lizards in this special place."

A lesbian couple, without recording a word about the ruin, had used the register to broadcast a tirade against the rednecks who persecuted them: some day, they avowed, the world would be ready for their kind of love. Something like half the entries, however, voiced an altogether different complaint—against cows. Grand Gulch, the centerpiece of Cedar Mesa, had been off-limits to cattle for more than twenty years. But in deference to more than a century of ranching in this part of Utah, the BLM had been reluctant to close off the other canyons to livestock. On the hike up the side-canyon to Monarch, we had stepped over a few old cow pies.

The tree huggers and self-styled environmentalists who used the register to voice their feelings were outraged by this compromise with their sense of the sublime. Out loud, I read one diatribe against the BLM after another. The cows threatened the ruin, grazed the bushes to stubble, shat on the trail, and drank from the water tank. It was high time the BLM pulled its head out of its ass and banned livestock from every canyon on Cedar Mesa and Comb Ridge.

I hadn't thought Greg was listening, but now he walked up, laid down his camera, and said, "Gimme that register." Sitting down on the bedrock, he scribbled his own entry. When I read it, I collapsed in a paroxysm of gut-wrenching hysterics—a fit very like the one that had seized all three of us beside the Chinle spring on the evening of September 7, when I had read the tragicomic passage from *Traders to the Navajos* out loud.

Greg was, I knew, one of the least PC guys I had ever met. His Aussie iconoclasm was wont to open fire with both barrels against righteous homilies of all sorts. But in those few moments with the register, he had penned a riff so inspired that I would have given much to watch the reactions on the faces of the next twenty or thirty visitors who read it. Greg wrote:

> *Hi,*
> *I am a cow. I wandered up here to take a shit + nibble on the grass, + wash off in the spring. I was aghast to pick up the book and read all the nasty things you people write about us cows. Listen, you fucks, don't ya eat burgers? And if you're gonna fence us cows out, how about people, lesbians, and arkyologists? I say cows built this fortress. Go dig up the ruin. You'll find our bones!*
> *—Moo.*

By that evening, we were camped most of the way up another side-canyon, on graceful, sinuous shelves of stone beside two crystalline pothole pools. Just two hundred yards farther up the canyon we had visited a diminutive ruin, one far less known than Monarch—not a very prepossessing site, except for one utterly beguiling detail. On the wall of the main structure, head-high, someone had lifted a baby to print its footprint in the muddy mortar. More than seven hundred years later, that playful signature still testified to the capacity for whimsy in a people who may have been facing the daily threat of starvation, the dread of enemy attack.

It was a happy evening. In fourteen days, we'd hiked, by my reckoning, exactly one hundred miles. We were only seven miles as the crow flies south of the second roadcut, where Highway 95 connected Blanding to Cedar Mesa. Two moderate days, another resupply and reunion, and then two or three more days to the end of our trek. Nothing, it seemed, but the most perverse bad luck could now stop us from completing the first traverse of the Comb Ridge.

LAST DAYS

STOPPING AT MONARCH CAVE HAD SET me to ruminating on the toll that more than a century and a quarter of visitation had taken on the irreplaceable ruins of the Southwest. Vaughn and I had often shared the rueful fantasy of what it must have been like to hike down Grand Gulch in the 1890s, when the Wetherills, McLoyd, and Graham had been the first Anglos to poke through those pristine cliff dwellings, to dig without compunction in the dirt and pack out artifacts by the thousands.

Every generation of adventurers, of course, is convinced that it was born too late. At the end of the nineteenth and the beginning of the twentieth centuries, as explorers set out for the North and South Poles, some of them wondered out loud about the uselessness to mankind of their arbitrary goals. But they had been born too late to explore the Far West or search for the source of the Nile. There were only the world's most sterile places left to discover: the highest mountains, the most lifeless deserts, the wastes of ice and snow stretching across the Arctic and the Antarctic. Today, we look back on the years from 1890 to 1920 as the golden age of polar exploration. Nansen and Peary, Scott and Shackleton and Amundsen are hallowed heroes, and the modern adventurer who knows that he can book a commercial trip to sky dive over the North Pole or coast the Antarctic Peninsula in a cruise ship wonders what's left out there to keep the game fresh.

Five or six years before, Vaughn had taken me to a very obscure part of Cedar Mesa, to see a site he had recently discovered. He had nicknamed it the Pottery Shrine. Across an otherwise unremarkable bench below a small cliff was spread the most dazzling array of potsherds I had ever seen in one place. Along with plain and corrugated grayware, there were many black-and-white Mesa Verde sherds, as well as Tusayan polychrome painted in thick bands of orange, red, and black. The scattering was so rich that Vaughn speculated that the bench might have been a special location for the Anasazi, even a shrine—a place perhaps where they had come deliberately to break pots, "retiring" them in a ceremony full of meanings we can no longer divine.

But then, shortly after my visit, Vaughn took Winston Hurst to the Pottery Shrine. Instead of oohing and aahing, as I had, Winston took one look and said wearily, "Yeah, when I was a kid every place out here looked like that."

Several months after our Comb Ridge trip, I had a talk with Winston. He confirmed Vaughn's tale of his visit to the Pottery Shrine, adding, "What's amazing is that a place like that is amazing anymore."

Growing up in Blanding, Winston had had the northern end of the Comb Ridge—the very sector we were traversing on September 14 and 15—as a backyard playground. He had first become acquainted with the ridge as a young boy, around 1954, when his father had taken him out to watch workers blast the first auto road across the northern Comb. Long since fallen into disuse, its western ramp diagonaling down the precipice undriveable today, that road is referred to now as the Old Dugway.

Winston had first camped below the Comb as a Boy Scout at age thirteen. He quickly fell in love with the place. As soon as he could drive, he started spending many days of his teenage years hiking its side-canyons, often alone, as he made his own discoveries of dozens of Anasazi sites. "There was hardly anybody else out there then," Winston reminisced. "If I ever saw another vehicle in Butler Wash, I'd be amazed. I always carried a shovel. The road was just an old two-track snaking down the wash. I'd have to rebuild it every trip.

"Every single site, there was so much more stuff on the ground back then. Since the early '60s, there's been a continuous and steady disappearance of potsherds. People just high-grade the biggest and spiffiest pieces. Where there used to be hundreds of painted sherds and stone tools, now there's only flakes and grayware. It's hard to exaggerate the change."

All over the Southwest, but especially in towns like Blanding, a time-honored tradition prevailed as late as the 1960s. On a Sunday afternoon, boys would go out to search for arrowheads, or a whole family might dig in a ruin looking for pots. "When I grew up," Winston recalled, "that kind of thing was so routine. I didn't know until I went to college and enrolled in an archaeology class that it was illegal to dig on public land. Everybody did a little digging, including me. While I was still in high school, a friend and I found a site in Recapture Creek where stuff was eroding out of the ground. We hauled out two skeletons and a small pot, threw it all in a gunny sack, and carried it home.

"My friend got the pot and I got the bones—which is sort of appropriate, since I would become an archaeologist who's more interested in the people than in their things. The bones ended up on a shelf in Mom's storage closest, next to her canned pears. She finally had a friend get rid of them."

At Brigham Young University, where he majored in anthropology, Winston first learned that his adolescent play had violated the Antiquities Act of 1906. But, as he is quick to clarify, "In the early '60s, we weren't doing hard-core pothunting. There were guys for whom digging was a serious hobby and a competitive sport, but it wasn't for economic gain. It wasn't until the mid-1970s, with the growing notion that it was a good thing to invest in antiques and gold, that a real black market for antiquities popped up. Then the government started to crack down. And that made people think, 'In a few years, nobody'll be able to dig, so we better go out and dig like a son-of-a-bitch now.'"

Back from BYU (and from graduate school at Eastern New Mexico University), Winston realized that his new archaeological ethics put him at odds with some of the Blanding friends he had grown up with. Meanwhile, serious pothunting continued apace through the 1980s and 1990s, much of it carried out by Blanding men. The most brazen was Earl Shumway, who bragged in 1988 that he had lost count of the number of sites on public land that he had vandalized over the years, but that it was in the thousands. He also swore that the odds of his getting caught were one in a million.

In 1995, however, Shumway was prosecuted for violating the Archaeological Resources Protection Act. The charges included the allegation that he had looted, from a remote site in Canyonlands National Park, the remains of an infant wrapped in a ceremonial blanket. Shumway was not caught red-handed: rather, it was DNA from a cigarette butt he had left at the scene of the crime that clinched the case. "Perhaps the most notorious archaeological thief in American history," as the *Los Angeles Times* called him, Shumway was sentenced to five years in the federal penitentiary—the longest prison term yet meted out in the United States for vandalizing a prehistoric site.

Yet by 2004, high-tech pothunting was still going on all over the Southwest. The most ambitious grave-robbers are known to use helicopters and armed bodyguards to abet their crimes. To unearth the pots that fetch the highest prices on the black market, vandals routinely use backhoes and even bulldozers to plow through the ruins, tossing aside even human skeletons to get at their booty.

The United States remains one of the few countries in the world in which it is legal to dig antiquities on private land. That benighted proviso serves as a tragically convenient loophole for the pothunters. Even such prestigious auction houses as Sotheby's and Christie's still traffic in prehistoric treasures. Several times I had searched the eBay website for Anasazi pots, sickened at what I found—each vessel annotated with the disclaimer that a certificate proved the object had been dug on private land. (These certificates, of course, are pathetically easy to fake.)

Back in Blanding, where he became a curator at the Edge of the Cedars Museum, Winston occasionally found himself the object of homegrown antagonisms. Not a sanctimonious fellow—as I knew, Winston would be the last person to preach backcountry ethics to some former high school buddy—he nonetheless, as a professional archaeologist, stood for values that were anathema to the Blanding good old boys. "Yeah," he told me, "I've had some episodes when the tensions ran high. I've gotten flipped off. Nasty comments in the grocery store line. But only once did I get screamed at nose-to-nose."

I asked Winston whether the digging by the Illustrated American Exploring Expedition in 1892 had constituted, in his view, simple pothunting. "At least the IAEE and the Wetherills kept some kind of documentation of what they found," he answered. He went on to tell me a dolorous rumor of true pothunting—by no less a figure than a government employee—from the turn of the twentieth century. "T. Mitchell Prudden comes through here around 1900. He hires Charles Lang to guide him." Prudden was an amateur archaeologist from the

East who made several important intellectual breakthroughs in the study of the Anasazi; Lang was a photographer who had served on several of Richard Wetherill's expeditions. "They jog along on their mules. Prudden writes down in his diary what Lang tells him. They get to Comb Wash, where Lang starts talking about some guy named Gaines, a government surveyor. 'Gaines dug here,' Lang says, pointing out a ruin. 'Gaines dug there.' Over and over. The trouble is, we have no idea who Gaines was.

"The act of documenting the provenience of their finds," Winston went on, "no matter how informally or generally, is what separates people like the Wetherills and the IAEE guys from people like Gaines. I hesitate to call what they did good archaeology, but at least they left us enough information so that their collections can still be found and studied and, in many cases, connected to a place on the land."

On the evening of September 14, in our high-canyon camp beside the clear pools, the temperature finally dropped appreciably. The night was the coolest since the storm of September 4. I wore my felt cap to bed, and pulled my lightweight sleeping bag up around my neck.

The next morning, we stuck to the crest of the Comb once more. We had passed north of the central stretch, so rich in ruins, entering terrain that even Vaughn didn't know so well. Skirting a low cliff on the west side, I stumbled upon a graffito scratched in the rock by a disgruntled hunter more than sixty years ago:

Kayenta, Arizona
LOOKING FOR DAMN BUCK
Allen Kneal
3/21/42

Once more, here on the crest, the vestiges of the ancients were minimal. Yet at 11:00 AM, we came across one of the more puzzling sites of our whole journey. On skimpy ledges partway up a reddish buttress thrusting south, we found three tall walls festooned with loopholes. Each took a slightly tricky climb to get to, but the curious fact was that none of the walls enclosed a space big enough for a person to lie down in. "Weird, hyper-defensive," I wrote in my journal. The structures were neither granaries nor dwellings. Were they simply lookout posts, sentry boxes for spying on an enemy creeping along the ridge crest from the south? If so, where was the village they guarded? Once more, the terror of the thirteenth century spoke in the mute ambiguity of collapsing walls made of stones and mud.

That day, we ran another gauntlet of endless ups and downs, though the Comb's teeth and notches here were not quite so fierce as they had been two days before and ten miles farther south. Again, we could find no water in the dried-up potholes near the ridge top. Relatively early, about 2:00 PM, we decided to plunge off the crest to the east to look for water and a campsite.

And once more, the choice of where to spend the night sparked a minor tiff. Greg found the first tank with water in it, low on an eastern bench of the Comb. It was not a very appealing spot, but for all we knew, that tank might be the only water we could find. I suggested dropping our packs here while we scouted around for a better camp. In answer, Vaughn charged off in one direction, Greg in another. I followed, annoyed.

At last Greg found us better water and a nicer camp. As we sat in the shade of a juniper, I tried to voice my displeasure with the process of decision making. Vaughn's answers only riled me further. "I knew we'd find a better campsite down here," he said, and, "I guess I think I know where to find water."

"That's not the point," I rejoined. "It's the process that bugs me." Vaughn didn't respond.

Over dinner that evening, I lapsed into a glum, reflective mood. On every expedition I had ever been on, there came a point at which my teammates and I grew so used to each other's constant company that we stopped being curious about each other. Conversations shrank to logistical details. Once-innocuous habits and quirks on another's part started to seem like aggravations. It was, I knew, a kind of cabin fever. It might pass or it might persist: but I feared that we had reached that point on the Comb Ridge.

Since we were camped a mere three and a half miles south of the Highway 95 roadcut, with another resupply scheduled for the next afternoon, we lolled late in our sleeping bags, enjoying the fresh, cool morning of September 16. Our 9:30 start was the tardiest yet of our sixteen days on the Comb, and that leisurely stroll toward the highway the gentlest march of the whole traverse.

We reached the roadcut at 2:00 PM. Once more, a canyon with

its black asphalt ribbon laid a sinister barrier across our path. We sat down on a shoulder only twenty feet above the highway, as cars whizzed through the artificial gap without their drivers noticing us.

The Old Dugway that crossed the Comb five miles farther north had at least had a certain logic about it, as it followed an Indian trail that slanted up a steep couloir on the west, where the Comb uncharacteristically turned and doubled back on itself. Highway 95, in contrast, had been dynamited through the ridge in a place where no trail had ever existed. Staring at the intrusive blacktop, I was reminded of a phrase from W. H. Auden's poem, "Et in Arcadia Ego," in which, musing on rural Austria (where he owned a summer house), he observes "How the autobahn / Thwarts the landscape / In godless Roman arrogance."

Later Winston Hurst would annotate for me the history of this roadcut, which had been carved through the Comb around 1970. "I thought they did it just to personally piss me off," he said sardonically. "It was all about boats and Winnebagos going to Lake Powell. I heard from a BLM official that the highway department put the road there just because they liked the way it looked."

Renée and Ariann showed up at 3:00 PM, straight from another long drive down from Castle Valley. Renée brought snacks for all three of us—Dorito chips and salsa, homemade brownies so rich they gave us sugar buzzes—and a couple of six-packs of 3.2 Budweiser. Greg spent many a long moment holding Ariann in his arms and cooing nonsense syllables to his baby. Marcia did not arrive until 5:30, after getting off work at Edge of the Cedars Museum. Dinner for the night was bulging sandwiches from Subway in Blanding, arguably the finest cuisine available in one of the most gustatorially challenged towns in all of Utah. At least Marcia had had the foresight to pack a cooler with more Tecate and Moosehead from the Far Out fridge in Bluff.

Leery of causing another disruption in the rhythm of our long march, our kindly resuppliers bade us goodbye around 10:00 PM. Vaughn and Greg scuttled down into a little hollow to the south, out of sight of the highway, to pitch their tents, while out of sheer inertia I pitched mine right on the shelf where we had dropped our packs in the afternoon. In the middle of the night, several semis whining up the grade woke me, and once, when I went out to pee, I ran smack into a barbed wire fence designed to keep cows meandering up out of Butler Wash from blundering to a bloody death on Route 95.

The first thing Vaughn said in the morning was, "I hate resupply.

Especially Budweiser." Later he admitted to feeling the worst he had any day on the trip.

"Are you trying to tell us you've got a genuine hangover?" I teased.

"Pissed me off." It was one of Vaughn's pat phrases, useful for all kinds of occasions. (Another was, "Beats the hell outa me.")

"How many beers did you drink?"

"Seven or eight. But four of 'em were those cow-piss 3.2 Buds."

For all the woes of resupply, at the roadcut we had stocked up on the necessary gear, food, and water to see us through to the end of the Comb, a mere fifteen miles ahead by my reckoning from the maps. Greg had swapped out some eight pounds of camera gear for a fluffy little pillow that belonged to Ariann.

Highway 95 makes a long swooping bend to the south as it cuts through the Comb. In doing so, it executes an end run around a sharp, soaring, multi-summitted fin, the closest thing after the Mule Ear to a genuine pinnacle along the Comb. Winston Hurst had told me that that formation, visible from miles away on all sides, was known to both the Utes and the Navajo as the Mountain Sheep's Testicles. I also knew that it had been an Anasazi refuge.

In only half an hour on the morning of September 17, we circled the Testicles on the east and emerged on a high saddle just north of the tower. There we dropped our packs, as we prepared to scramble to the top.

All of a sudden, I felt extremely dizzy. Staring at Cedar Mesa in the west, I actually saw double for a few minutes. Two years before, I had suffered a three-week bout of vertigo that left me reeling and nauseated. At its worst, I found it scary even to ride my bicycle around the streets of Cambridge. The vertigo had come on like this, all of a sudden, in the middle of a day with Greg on Cedar Mesa, as we scrambled up cliffs to reach an inaccessible dwelling. Could this be a recurrence? If so, what a miserable way to end the trip!

Now I told my friends what was I was feeling.

"Maybe you're having a stroke," Greg jibed in his gruff way.

"Don't even joke about it."

In the end, the dizziness lasted for only about five hours, until it gradually ebbed away. I would never figure out what had caused it, but through the rest of the morning and into the afternoon, I fantasized hypochondriacally. A spider bite? Some hallucinogen baked into those sugary brownies?

Meanwhile, climbing the mini-towers of the Mountain Sheep's Testicles, I had to watch my balance with extra vigilance, for fear of lurching off the precipice to the west. Near the top of the strange sandstone gendarme, we found low masoned and dry-laid walls facing east and south, enclosing ill-defined spaces. Were these more look-out posts? Winston Hurst had ventured the opinion that the place was a "retreat" of some kind. If so, had it served the Utes as well as the Anasazi? Scatterings of sherds and flakes proved the presence of the Old Ones here, but some of the defensive walls looked to be of more recent manufacture. As we descended, we tucked one more Comb Ridge enigma into our mental belts.

At 10:00 AM, two miles farther along the crest, we came to the top of Posey's Trail, where a path both prehistoric and historic made its way up the west side of the Comb by a devious and clever zig-zag. Cribwork along its upper bends testified to twentieth-century improvements in the old crossing trail.

Vaughn pointed to an isolated mesa some four miles to the south-west, a kind of satellite plateau in front of the higher, much larger Cedar Mesa. "That's just covered with PI sites," he said. "Winston gave me the tour." The Pueblo I period, from about AD 750 to 900, had proved the most elusive of all for Anasazi scholars to pin down. Unlike the gloomy Basketmaker alcoves, with their upright-slab cists and pithouses, their magnificent rock art, or the dramatic cliff dwell-ings of Pueblo III, Pueblo I sites were typically small "unit pueb-los"—a mere four to six contiguous rooms, made of crude masonry or fugitive daub-and-wattle, built on open benches where the storms of the subsequent centuries reduced them to rubble. It would take the pioneering 1940s work of Harvard archaeologist J. O. Brew, survey-ing Alkali Ridge, a long mesa east of Blanding, to put PI firmly on the map, demonstrating in the same stroke that the early Basketmakers and the later Pueblo culture were one and the same people.

"And that," Vaughn added, still pointing at the satellite mesa, "is where Posey died."

———— ∞∞∞ ————

Posey's War, called by some the last Indian war ever waged in the United States, was not really a war. It was instead the final sorry epi-sode in a four-decades-long chronicle of conflict between Mormons and some of the last free-roaming Indians in the country. At the time of the Hole-in-the-Rock expedition of 1879–80, southeastern Utah and southwestern Colorado were the homeland of an assortment of Ute tribes and of their distant cousins, the Paiutes. Once the Mormons had gotten their toehold at Bluff, and then expanded their domain to Bluff and Monticello, the indigenes found their immemorial liberty threatened at every hand.

To resolve the conflict, the U.S. government established the Ute Mountain Ute Reservation in 1895, with headquarters at Towaoc, Colorado. But the Indians consigned to that tract were mostly Weminuche Utes, who were not always on easy terms with other Utes farther west or with the San Juan Paiutes, who even today lack a reservation of their own. (Confined largely to a pair of communities on the Navajo Reservation, the San Juan Paiutes were not formally recognized as a tribe by the U.S. government until 1989.)

From 1880 on, but especially after the Mormons took up ranching in favor of farming, the settlers' intrusion upon the homeland of the Utes and Paiutes proved incompatible with the hunter-gatherer lifestyle the non-reservation Indians continued to practice. As deer and elk grew scarcer, Mormon cattle and horses proved tempting prey. Especially around Blanding, the settlers raised a hue and cry about finding a solution to the "Indian problem."

In 1915 a man named Tse-ne-gat—historians today cannot determine whether he was a Paiute or a Ute—was accused of killing a Mexican sheepherder. When a local sheriff and then a U.S. marshal out of Salt Lake City tried to arrest Tse-ne-gat, a band of Utes and Paiutes refused to deliver him. After fighting a battle near Bluff, the band retreated to the rugged wilderness north of Navajo Mountain—the same fastness where Hoskinini had eluded Kit Carson's troops in 1863–64 but a Paiute refuge long before the Navajos had appropriated it.

Hoping to resolve this impasse, the U.S. Army sent Gen. Hugh Lenox Scott from Virginia all the way out to Utah to apprehend the miscreant. In Bluff, however, John and Louisa Wetherill interceded. Louisa was firmly convinced of Tse-ne-gat's innocence, and John had won the Paiutes' trust to the extent that now he was able to send a message to Navajo Mountain that succeeded in luring Tse-ne-gat and three of his allies out of hiding.

Scott's soldiers and the four "renegades" traveled by motorcar first to Salt Lake City and then to Denver for trial, capturing newspaper headlines well beyond the Southwest. Louisa Wetherill dug up witnesses to testify on Tse-ne-gat's behalf, and attended the Denver trial herself, where Tse-ne-gat won a quick acquittal.

The verdict stuck in the Mormon craw. As Gary Topping writes in his excellent history of the region, *Glen Canyon and the San Juan Country*, "Tse-ne-gat was a handsome and charismatic person whose journey to Salt Lake City and Denver had been almost a triumphal tour, and many San Juan settlers suspected that he had duped both press and jury with a 'noble Indian' image."

There followed eight years of simmering tensions between the free Indians in southeast Utah and the residents of Bluff and Blanding. Posey's War was triggered in March 1923, when two Utes were arrested for robbing a sheep camp, killing a calf, and burning a bridge. They stood trial in Blanding, where they were convicted.

Posey was a Paiute man who had married into a Ute band that roamed west of Blanding. By 1923, at about sixty years old, he had been involved in a number of previous fracases between Mormons and Indians. In historian Robert McPherson's words, Posey had "become the symbol of this mutual antagonism" and gained "a reputation for arrogance and thievery." During the mere three hours between the verdict and sentencing—a delay required by the Blanding Mormons' need to eat lunch—Posey helped the two Utes escape. In the confrontation, a witness later reported, one of the Utes managed to seize the sheriff's gun and, even as he rode away on the back of Posey's horse, turn and fire a bullet that struck the sheriff's horse in the neck.

The Blanding men formed a posse. According to Topping's account, the chagrined sheriff now told the posse, "Every man here is deputized to shoot. I want you to shoot everything that looks like an Indian."

Once more, the mixed band of Utes and Paiutes loyal to Posey fled southwest toward Navajo Mountain. Word of the "war" spread like wildfire, reaching newspapers as far away as Chicago. Posey briefly captured the public imagination as Geronimo had in the last few months before his final surrender in 1886.

As the fleeing Utes and Paiutes crossed Comb Ridge—probably on Posey's Trail, where Greg, Vaughn, and I now took a rest break and pondered history—Posey paused to serve as a rear guard holding the posse at bay while his people negotiated the dangerous descent of the Comb on the west. A lucky shot struck Posey in the hip, causing a wound from which he would eventually die, as he tried to hole up somewhere on the satellite mesa across Comb Wash that Vaughn had pointed out to us.

Indian messengers later filtered back to Blanding with the news that Posey was dead. According to Topping, the San Juan authorities refused to believe the report, "and the body had to be exhumed no less than three times before all parties were satisfied." A U.S. marshal examining Posey's body declared the cause of death to be blood poisoning from the hip wound, but, according to McPherson, "the Utes believed Posey died from poisoned Mormon flour."

The upshot of this last armed conflict in Utah between Native Americans and white settlers was the creation, before the year was out, of the White Mesa Ute Reservation. On that small tract of hard-grazed plateau, only seven miles south of Blanding, some of the descendants of the final fugitive band live today. As Topping wrote in 1997, "In the mythology of San Juan County, the Posey War occupies a place equal to the Hole-in-the-Rock expedition, and virtually every old-timer in Blanding has some kind of recollection of the incident and will talk about it enthusiastically."

McPherson captures the surreal anachronism of this tragic, unequal showdown. In his words, the Blanding Mormons "mobilized quickly and combined frontier know-how with World War I warfare techniques. Talk of electrified fences and aircraft armed with machine guns and bombs, the use of a prisoner stockade, . . . combined with using automobiles to track Indians, horse-mounted posses, and old-fashioned gunfights made this event dramatic if not unique."

———— ⬦ ————

Pushing on north, we made fast time, as the Comb, succumbing to geological exhaustion, leveled out, its teeth here only worn-down lumps of broken sandstone. For the first time, we hiked consistently at or above 6000 feet. The bare slickrock of the hundred-plus miles behind us here gave way to stands of piñon and juniper, in places almost thick enough to suggest a forest.

Yet here, for the only time on our whole hike, we hiked parallel to an old four-wheel-drive road that trundled up the Comb from the east. On the Navajo Reservation, we had seen not a single footprint. Now, suddenly, we strode across the looping tracks of ATVs and dirt bikes. Vaughn in particular could not hide his disgust. "Looks like the bubbas really went to town here," he muttered. If ever we needed an object lesson in just how accessible and how vulnerable to thoughtless vehicular recreation the Comb Ridge was, we got it in those few miles near the forest road.

The brief cool spell had come and gone: now the temperature was back up in the high 80s. As we had on almost every day of our trip, we hiked in shorts and tee shirts. We had expected the last fifteen miles of the Comb to take three days, but now we realized that with a good push today, we could finish the traverse on the morrow. We sailed along. I felt a twinge of sorrow at the thought that I had finally gotten into the best shape I'd been in in decades—my heavy pack no longer an unwelcome burden, just a fact of ambulatory life—only to contemplate the prospect of slipping, once the trip was over, back into the sedentary torpor of a winter in front of the word processor back in Cambridge.

We stopped to camp at 4:00 PM, having found a near-perfect grove among the piñons right on the crest of the Comb, atop a 6200-foot knob that overlooked South Whiskers Draw. We had covered ten miles, not a herculean deed, but still the longest day's march yet on our trek. It was our first camp on the crest since the camp among the giant potholes on September 9—the first chance to see a real sunset in more than a week. The equinox was due in only four more days. Expiring in a golden haze, the sun sank below Cedar Mesa at 7:20 PM. It had been rising the last few mornings between 7:05 and 7:10 AM.

We were only five miles from the end of our traverse. Once more, I got out the sat phone to revise our pickup for a day earlier than planned. It would be fitting, I thought, to do something to make our last evening special, so I suggested, "Maybe if the breeze dies down, we could build a fire."

But Vaughn was not in a celebratory mood. "I don't want to burn down the forest on our last night out," he rejoined, vetoing my whim.

After dinner, we sat around a cold stove rather than a warm fire. Vaughn and Greg engaged in a long discussion of Bluff politics—the water board, the sewer system, feuds among longtime neighbors. As the resident of a comparably tiny Utah town, Greg could relate, but I had nothing to contribute.

We were all three in bed by 9:30. There was no getting around the sense that the end of our marathon hike felt like an anticlimax. In my journal I wrote, "I'm sorry to say it, but I'll just be glad to get this trip over with. The tension between Vaughn and me hasn't gone away. It's always under the surface. It's a shame—it's made the trip a lot less fun than it should have been. Greg is a curiously neutral and flexible middle man, though he leans toward Vaughn on most things."

I woke at 4:30 AM, unable to fall back to sleep. Venus shone bright, high in the morning sky. The malaise hung leaden upon my spirit. At last I had linked it to my sister's death, six months before. Now I recalled the last "hike" I had taken with Jenny, one January day in the hallways of Boulder's Community Hospital, as, with slow, uncertain steps, hanging onto my arm, dragging her oxygen tube behind her, she paced several dozen yards down the carpeted corridor and back. The journey exhausted her, and she crawled back under the covers of her bed with a hopeless sigh.

At the time, as Jenny held my arm, I had flashed back to a hike up Green Mountain we had taken when I was twenty and she seventeen. With her best friend, Barb, Jenny had made a kind of game out of the descent: the two of them would pretend to lose control on the steep, gravelly trail, accelerating into a reckless jog, until they ran into a spruce or pine that arrested their flight. All three of us laughed so hard, tears came to our eyes.

In the hospital, the tears had come again, forty years later, though I had stifled them for Jenny's sake. Now, lying in my sleeping bag, staring at Venus, listening to the soft breeze ruffle the piñon branches, I let the tears flow without trying to stanch them.

For our last day on the Comb, we had one more important stop to make—at Richard Wetherill's Cave 7 in North Whiskers Draw. That small alcove, fortuitously placed only a mile from our pickup spot, had been the scene where one of the greatest discoveries in the prehistory of the Southwest had been made. Yet so obscure was that recess among the seldom-visited bends of Whiskers Draw, that after Wetherill's untimely death in 1910—he was murdered by a Navajo in Chaco Canyon in a still-mysterious incident—the location of Cave 7 had been lost for eight decades.

As we set out at 7:30 AM, I was keenly looking forward to exploring the alcove, which I had visited only once before, some eleven years ago, when I was just beginning to indulge my curiosity about the Old Ones.

By late morning, we had reached the top of a hill that, at 6521 feet, marked our highest elevation on the traverse as well as the northern terminus of the Comb. Then we headed down a steep ridge and slope toward North Whiskers Draw.

All morning dark clouds had been amassing in the west. Now, as we angled off the ridge, rain began to fall—the first rain, but for a couple of intermittent spatters, in the last fourteen days. It was a soft, gentle, steady rain—a female rain, as the Navajo would call it.

Once we had entered North Whiskers Draw, we hiked down the dry streambed between high arroyo banks that blocked our view of the slopes sheltering the canyon. On my own, I would have been hard put to find Cave 7, but Vaughn remembered the way. At the appropriate bend, we climbed the right-hand arroyo bank, crossed a grassy island that had once been an Anasazi cornfield, clambered down into a tight side-arroyo, pushed through scratchy scrub oak and dodged poison ivy, and then came abruptly upon the alcove.

At first glance, it was not much to look at. The alcove was about one hundred feet broad but only fifteen feet deep, with a low ceiling that gave the place a cramped air. Adding to the aura of gloominess was the fact that the hollow under the leaning sandstone cliff faced west-northwest: it would receive, at most, a little late-afternoon sunlight in summer. The only visible structure was a single wall, ten feet long by four feet high, crudely masoned out of unshaped stones glued together with a yellowish mud.

Yet this was Wetherill's long-lost Cave 7.

Spurred by the growing competition for antiquities posed not only by such fellow ranchers as McLoyd and Graham but by the massively sponsored Illustrated American Exploring Expedition, Wetherill set out in December 1893 on an ambitious program to explore canyons he had never previously entered. As usual, the exigencies of running the Mancos ranch restricted his field time to the dead of winter—with its short days and frozen ground by far the hardest season to dig in the ruins. By now, Wetherill too had won prestigious eastern sponsorship, that of B. Talbot Hyde and his brother Fred Hyde Jr., heirs to the Bab-O Soap fortune. With an amateur interest of their own in archaeology, piqued by an 1892 visit to the Wetherills' ranch, the Hydes were readily convinced to bankroll the 1893 expedition and to donate its finds to the American Museum of Natural History (AMNH).

A dingy hollow in the wall and a dwelling, near Cave 7

From Bluff, Wetherill's team set out for Grand Gulch, where McLoyd and Graham had already made great discoveries three winters before. But on the way to Cedar Mesa, the team took a long detour north up Butler Wash.

In a letter dated December 17, Wetherill excitedly announced to Talbot Hyde, "Our success has surpassed all expectations." In one alcove, the team had made what Wetherill liked to think was "the most valuable find in the History of America." The heading of that letter, a cryptic formula, would prove critical in relocating Cave 7 almost a century later: "First Valley Cottonwood Creek 30 Miles North Bluff City."

In Cave 7, Wetherill's team had dug through the unpromising two-room cliff dwelling on the surface, in the process partially destroying it. "We found nothing in the rooms," the self-taught archaeologist later wrote, though large ceramic pots were found buried elsewhere in the alcove. Only a hunch kept Wetherill from giving up on the ruin and moving on to the next site. A number of versions of that hunch have come down to us, mostly in the later recollections of others in the party, including Richard's brothers John and Al. At the bottom of the trench that the team had dug in the cliff-dweller ruin, someone—probably Richard or John—noticed a "discoloration of the sand." The team dug deeper, persisting through three feet of sterile yellow sand that yielded no further traces of occupation.

Then, abruptly, the shovel began to unearth human remains. In a frenzy of discovery, the team dug on, until the cavity in the floor of the alcove was deeper than a man stood tall. By the end of their labor, the diggers had uncovered more than ninety skeletons. Some of the dead had been buried in rows, knees flexed, surrounded by grave goods. Yet far more of the skeletons were strewn about in disorder. And Wetherill noticed a chilling fact. "Many of the skulls are broken," he wrote later, "as well as the ribs, and the bones of the arms and legs. In the backbones of two different skeletons we found the ends of spear points firmly embedded." The conclusion was inescapable: Wetherill's team had come upon the remains of a massacre or mass execution. (The dead found in formal burials may have belonged to a separate episode, or they could have been victims whom their relatives returned to inter with proper dignity.)

At least as interesting as the signs of carnage was the fact that associated with these skeletons found so deep in the soil was not a single piece of pottery but instead abundant "feather cloth and baskets" as well as stone pipes. The key observation Wetherill made was that the skulls of these dead looked different from those of the cliff dwellers he had dug up elsewhere. The crania of the latter were flattened in the back, whereas the skulls of the massacre victims were fully rounded. In that very first letter to Talbot Hyde, Wetherill concluded, "They are a different race from anything I have ever seen."

Wetherill called these long-ago dead the "Basket People." The term was soon regularized to "Basketmaker"—an appellation the rancher never really liked, for, as he knew, virtually every ancient tribe the world over had made baskets. Nevertheless, the term has stuck.

The profound intellectual breakthrough that Wetherill applied to his find seems routine today, but in 1893, it was far from a given conclusion. Because the Basket People lay much deeper in the soil than the cliff dwellers, Wetherill deduced that his "different race" had flourished during an earlier era.

Six decades later, Alfred V. Kidder, the great archaeologist who had convened the first Pecos Conference, during which the phases of Anasazi culture were defined, including Basketmaker II and III, tipped his hat to the Mancos rancher: "[Nels] Nelson and I have often been credited with doing the first stratigraphic work in the Southwest, but Richard, in recognizing the greater antiquity of the Basketmakers than that of the Cliff Dwellers, used the method many years before anyone else in that field."

Wetherill's assumption that the Basketmakers were a different race, a people subsequently driven out or extinguished by invading Puebloans (or Cliff Dwellers, as he called them), was a logical one. It held sway, in fact, for the next fifty years, until J. O. Brew on Alkali Ridge convincingly demonstrated the Basketmaker-Pueblo continuum. The different shapes of skulls, we now know, were caused by the artificial flattening of infants' crania by hard cradleboards first introduced during Pueblo times.

Wetherill bundled up his finds, skeletons and all, packed them back to Mancos, and arranged their shipment to New York with such perspicacity that ninety years later, physical anthropologist Christy G. Turner—the leading proponent of the controversial recent claims that Anasazi cannibalism was widespread—could examine the bones of sixty-one of the Cave 7 skeletons at the AMNH and reconfirm Wetherill's notion of a massacre or mass execution. Turner found no signs of cannibalism among these victims, but evidence for "perimortem damage"—physical insult at the time of death—was so pervasive that he could see no alternative to the conclusion that Cave 7 had once been the arena for an episode of unspeakable violence. Turner dated the event to sometime between 2500 and 1500 years ago.

Cave 7 was Wetherill's greatest discovery—one of the most important finds in the prehistoric Southwest. But after his premature death in 1910, the location of the alcove faded from human memory.

Because Wetherill went on that winter of 1893–94 to dig extensively in Grand Gulch and muddled his own taxonomy by starting a new cave-numbering system that duplicated the one from Butler Wash and Cottonwood Creek, Cave 7 was translated onto Cedar Mesa. In Frank McNitt's excellent 1957 biography, *Richard Wetherill: Anasazi*, a photo taken by the team in mid-excavation, with pots from the cliff dwellers and skulls from the Basketmakers lying in plain sight, was erroneously captioned "Basket Maker remains, discovered in Cave 7 during Richard Wetherill's 1897 Grand Gulch expedition."

By the 1980s, among devotees of the canyon country, Richard Wetherill had become something of a cult figure. But several generations of influential professionals went out of their way to denigrate the Wetherill brothers. Jesse Nusbaum, longtime superintendent of Mesa Verde National Park, characterized Richard's work there as "ravaging and looting" and "commercial exploitation" of the ruins. Nusbaum spread the canard that the brothers had used dynamite to excavate (no evidence for such explosive techniques on the Wetherills' part has ever come to light). Al Wetherill lived long enough to undergo a humiliating experience at Mesa Verde. At the age of eighty-four, he returned with his two grandsons in 1946 only to hear the ranger leading the tour of Cliff Palace spout Nusbaum-like aspersions on the brothers as ignorant pothunters. "Tell him, Pop. Set him straight," one of the grandsons pleaded—"Pop" being their fond nickname for the old man. "It's no use," Al muttered, keeping his silence.

The collections Richard Wetherill made over some fourteen years in the field, ranging from Mesa Verde to Cedar Mesa to Chaco Canyon, would eventually anchor the Southwest holdings of half a dozen major institutions, including not only the AMNH but Chicago's Field Museum and the Museum of the American Indian in New York as well. But by the 1980s, the few professionals who were well acquainted with those collections had little firsthand knowledge of the canyons from which they had come. Despite Wetherill's careful record keeping, many of his notes and photographs had been misplaced or lost. In general, the incredibly rich assemblages of artifacts and human remains that Wetherill had devoted the prime of his life to discovering and preserving had become detached from their proveniences—thereby robbing them of much of their potential power to cast light on Anasazi culture.

Starting in 1986, a small, close-knit group of avocational archaeologists conceived of a heady mission—to relink the alcoves in which

Richard Wetherill had dug with the collections he had sent to those eastern institutions. Calling themselves the Wetherill–Grand Gulch Research Project, the band was centered around Fred Blackburn, a feisty teacher, wilderness guide, amateur historian, and sometime rancher who lived in Cortez, Colorado. In the 1970s, Blackburn had served as a BLM ranger on Cedar Mesa. Hiking up and down Grand Gulch, he had developed an obsession with Richard Wetherill, whom he saw as a kindred soul. Vaughn himself, one of Fred's best friends, was a charter member of the project.

Fred had, in fact, been the central figure in my 1996 book about the Anasazi, *In Search of the Old Ones*, the Vergil to my Dante as I had started hiking through the canyons, making my own first discoveries of the ruins and rock art of the ancients. It was Fred who had introduced me to Vaughn, one day in 1994 on Cedar Mesa.

The project members had naively assumed that it would be a straightforward matter to go back east, enter the august museums, and be given free access to Wetherill's records and to the artifacts and human remains the rancher had dug so long ago. Many of the team's initial inquiries were coolly rebuffed. Among the project's staunch supporters, however, was one professional archaeologist—Winston Hurst. And gradually, as the team proved their seriousness, each member devoting hundreds of hours of volunteer labor to their passion, the museums' coolness thawed. Other highly respected professionals, including Arizona State University's Christy Turner and William Lipe of Washington State University, gave the project their imprimatur.

What the team members had to offer, above all, was a close familiarity with every bend of Grand Gulch. And almost at once, they made breakthroughs in relinking the artifacts with their proveniences. With copies of Wetherill's field notes and photographs in hand, Fred, Vaughn, and their cronies were able, for instance, to rediscover not only the alcove, but the very plot of dirt in the floor from which Wetherill had excavated such famous mummies as the Princess and Cut-in-Two Man. Fred himself coined the term for the apparently novel technique his team had begun to apply—"reverse archaeology."

The project's focus soon expanded well beyond Grand Gulch. Perhaps the most tantalizing challenge the team shouldered was to rediscover Wetherill's Cave 7, the site of the greatest discovery of his life. With his intimate knowledge of the wilderness just west of his home town of Blanding, Winston Hurst had long known that the Cave 7 of the Basketmaker massacre did not lie in Grand Gulch, or anywhere else on Cedar Mesa. The heading of Richard's breathless letter to Talbot Hyde—"First Valley Cottonwood Creek 30 Miles North Bluff City"—gave a strong though ambiguous clue. Cottonwood Creek heads high in the Abajo Mountains, flowing south some fifty miles to join the San Juan River just a mile west of Bluff. "30 Miles North Bluff City" narrowed the search further. But where was "First Valley"—a term that no longer sparked recognition in any of Blanding's old-timers?

Winston ransacked the writings of local historian Albert R. Lyman, son of one of the Hole-in-the-Rock pioneers, who had grown up in Bluff in the 1890s and moved to Blanding in 1905, and who happened to be Winston's great-uncle. Then he came across an interview Lyman had granted in 1973, shortly before his death. Asked where First Valley was, Lyman had answered, "First Valley is where you go over from the head of the Butler and enter the first valley you come to on the mountain." Winston deduced that "on the mountain" meant the lower slopes of Elk Ridge.

All these fugitive hints now pointed to Whiskers Draw. The name of that twin-branched drainage, demarcating the northern end of Comb Ridge, derives from a curious incident. Willard Butt, one of the Hole-in-the-Rock pioneers, had established a dairy farm near the mouth of that tributary of Cottonwood Creek. One evening an old Ute Indian, whom the Mormons had nicknamed Whiskers, showed up at the farm, pulled out a knife, and demanded that Butt serve him dinner. Thereafter, the canyon was known as Whiskers Draw.

The puzzle of Cave 7 had preoccupied the project since 1988, but it was only in 1990 that Winston and fellow project member Owen Severance started to push the search hard. They were greatly aided by a pair of photographs from the 1893 dig that a University of Pennsylvania archivist had sent Fred Blackburn. The searchers also had in hand copies of Wetherill's field notes and sketch of the cave.

As luck would have it, however, the true Cave 7 was the very last of all the alcoves in both South and North Whiskers Draw that the two men examined. Meanwhile, through months of dogged searching on Severance's part, he realized that he was getting warm, for dates scrawled in charcoal by Wetherill's team members on the walls of other alcoves started to cluster around December 17, 1893—the date of the revelatory letter from Richard to Talbot Hyde.

It was an afternoon in September 1990 when Winston and Owen

at last clinched the rediscovery. The moment he entered the alcove, Winston recognized the site, complete with the still-standing Pueblo III wall, as a perfect match for the 1893 photos. Fred learned of the finding of Cave 7 two days later when he pulled a postcard out of his mailbox in Cortez. Postmarked from Monticello, the card had neither salutation nor signature. It read simply "Bingo!"

The story of this marvelous latter-day detective case is laid out in full in *Cowboys & Cave Dwellers*, a popular account of the discovery and subsequent understanding of the Basketmakers in southeastern Utah, published in 1997 by Fred Blackburn and archaeoastronomer Ray Williamson. It is also covered in thorough scholarly detail in a brilliant professional paper, "Rediscovering the 'Great Discovery': Wetherill's First Cave 7 and Its Record of Basketmaker Violence," by Winston Hurst and Christy Turner, published in a 1993 BLM monograph called *Anasazi Basketmaker: Papers from the 1990 Wetherill-Grand Gulch Symposium*.

If ever reverse archaeology—the fledgling technique concocted by a band of amateurs in 1986 but by and large ignored as a resource by a previous century of deskbound academics—needed a banner to carry into the fray of theorizing about the prehistoric Southwest, the saga of the rediscovery of Cave 7 ought to fly high.

———— ∞ ————

With all this history in our heads, Vaughn, Greg, and I pushed through the scrub oak and walked into Cave 7 just before noon on September 18. In that instant, I experienced a double déjà vu, remembering the place from my own 1993 visit and from the old black-and-white photos shot during Wetherill's 1893 excavation.

We spent an hour inside the alcove. I could see why the 1990 searchers had for so long overlooked the place. "Such a dinky cave," I wrote in my journal—"you'd never guess such a great discovery could have happened here."

On the cliff above the single standing wall, we saw the charcoal signature "J L Ethridge"—long known to Vaughn and me as one of Wetherill's regular partners, the one most prone to leaving his immodest autograph in every alcove the team excavated. Toward the back of the alcove, we found a second Ethridge signature on a big slab on the ground that had evidently fallen from the ceiling. Later Fred

Blackburn would tell me that that slab had collapsed only a year or two after Winston and Owen had rediscovered Cave 7. On that jutting ceiling block, they had been able to photograph and record not only Ethridge's name, but the date December 20, 1893. On the fallen slab, the date was no longer visible.

Far less conspicuous, carved in a tiny hand on a boulder that stood in front of the ruin, was a neatly lettered "Wetherill 1893." So unobtrusive was this inscription that neither Winston nor Owen had noticed it on their first visit to Cave 7, nor had Fred—the most masterly decoder of historic signatures I had ever met—when his friends had returned with him several weeks after their rediscovery of the "great discovery." It was only years later that Fred had first detected the spidery inscription.

Staring into the dim recesses of the back of the cave, Greg saw what he at first thought was a curved piece of white pottery protruding from the dirt. When he picked it up, however, he was startled to hold the upper half of a human skull. "Hey, guys," he called to Vaughn and me, "come look at this!"

The skull was small, probably that of a child. The back of the

A skull, probably exposed by digging coyotes, and perhaps one of the many unfortunate residents of Cave 7 that Wetherill and his party excavated in 1893

cranium was round, not flattened. Here, evidently, was a last victim of the ancient massacre, still bearing witness to the catastrophe of more than 1500 years ago—a skull that not only Richard Wetherill had missed, but that all the subsequent visitors and pothunters had left in place.

Was this find a fitting finis to our long trek, or a ghoulish postscript? Yet as I held the object in my hand, there seemed nothing grotesque about it. The ages had bleached out all the tragedy from that porcelain crown of human bone. At last Greg carried the skull back to where he had found it, laid it on the ground, and covered it with several inches of dirt.

Our rendezvous on the old road winding up toward Elk Ridge was due in little more than an hour. We stepped out of Cave 7 and back into the female rain. Crossing North Whiskers Draw, we scrambled up the opposite arroyo bank, and then headed up the slope beyond. According to the map, the road was only half a mile away.

Here, as if to tantalize us with the sheer prehistoric abundance we were about to turn our backs on, the ground under our feet was covered with potsherds, many of them painted black-on-white and red-on-orange. Long after the Basketmakers had lived in Whiskers Draw, later Anasazi had flourished on its banks. We were tempted to stop and browse—no form of play in the canyon country had come to be more delightful to me than picking up potsherds, admiring them, and dropping them back on the ground—but we would have been late for our pickup.

Just before 1:00 PM, we struck the dirt road and walked half a mile east to a fork that I had scouted the week before we started our Comb traverse. There, for the last time, we dropped our packs. In eighteen days, we had traveled 125 miles. Within less than half an hour, our pickup van from Recapture Lodge would arrive.

Instead of relief or joy, I felt a vague sense of letdown. What could we possibly find in the upcoming months as compelling as each day's trudge, the regimen that had ruled our lives for the past two and a half weeks? I stared southwest at the knob that marked the end of the Comb and tried to visualize the ridge stretching all the way back to Kayenta. The start of our marathon hike seemed months in the past, not a mere eighteen days.

I sat down on my pack to wait. Yes, the end of the journey seemed anticlimactic. But a couple of hours earlier, as we had headed down from that terminal knob and the gentle rain had started to fall, Vaughn had abruptly stopped in his tracks, turned to Greg and me, and said,

"Thanks for hiking the Comb Ridge." He held out his hand. As I shook it, the tension between my old friend and me seemed to dissolve. I was deeply moved by Vaughn's gesture.

⚬⚬⚬

Back in Bluff, the rain poured down steadily for two days. Had we still been on the Comb, once more all our water problems would have been solved, as every dry pothole filled to the brim again. But we also might have had to wait days for our pickup, for the road that crossed Cottonwood Creek and angled up toward Elk Ridge was made of clay that turned as slick as ice after a rain. It might have taken two days of sun to dry the road adequately to drive it safely.

During the months after our trip, the sense of letdown that had assailed me as I dropped my pack for the last time modulated into a glow of accomplishment. There was, I knew by now, something quite predictable about the thud of anticlimax that attends the end of an expedition. In 1966, just hours after five of us had completed an arduous hike out to Rainy Pass Lodge from the Kichatna Spires, in an obscure corner of the Alaska Range—six days of hypothermic backpacking through a winter-struck wilderness in early October, after a full month of doing battle with unclimbed peaks—I had written an ambivalent last entry in my diary, "A good expedition, a successful one, and, for the most part, pleasant. Not an ordeal. . . . We never became a tight-knit group, but we remained friends."

Decades later, I look back on that expedition with unmitigated pride, tinged with nostalgia for meteoric youth, for during those five weeks in the range we made the first ascent of its highest peak, which we named Kichatna Spire. And if memory were not validation enough, in 2003, *Climbing* magazine hailed Kichatna Spire as the most difficult peak in North America—the hardest peak, that is, to climb by its easiest route, the route we had pioneered in September 1966.

Greg, Vaughn, and I would never expect any comparable encomium for having completed the first traverse (as far as we knew) of the Comb Ridge. We recognized that our deed could have been performed by many other men and women who might have put their minds to the task. Our success depended less on grit or perseverance than it did on savvy logistics and good luck (no injury worse than Greg's sprained ankle). Other adventurers in the past had gloated in print about their own landmark first traverses—of the Empty Quarter in the Arabian desert, for instance, or the glaciated wastes of Greenland. We would rest content to tip our caps to the curious happenstance that nobody seemed to have thought of traversing the Comb in a single push before 2004, a date by which almost every other naturally defined marathon hike in the contiguous United States had long since been executed backward, forward, and in record times.

For me, personally, the Comb Ridge journey served as a mellow, late-middle-aged answer to meteoric youth. There was gratification enough in the comments of several friends who, watching the slide show I later put together out of Greg's in-camera dupes, said in effect, "Pretty good for a sixty-one-year-old."

Ultimately, whatever pride I might feel at having completed the traverse is inextricable from the dozens—no, the scores—of moments of the most piercing happiness that came over me during those eighteen days, moments whose joy was all the keener for having shared them with two of my best friends. In Cambridge, chained to my word processor, I can pass weeks at a time that leave no imprint on my memory. What was I doing, say, in January 1999? I have not the foggiest idea. Even pleasant trips undertaken in the service of forgettable magazine articles—wine tasting my way through Burgundy in the footsteps of Thomas Jefferson, for instance, or animal watching from the back of a Bedford truck in the Serengeti—blur to a vague smudge of memory after a decade or so.

The Comb was different. For the rest of my life, those scores of enchanted moments—spotting the perfect gray-green arrowhead in the orange sand, finding the Basketmaker pictographs in the obscure north-facing alcove, laughing until our stomachs hurt at Hosteen Chee's deadpan confession in *Traders to the Navajos*, eating lunch on the tiny summit of the Mule Ear, wading the San Juan, staring at petroglyphs I thought I could almost comprehend, even holding the Basketmaker skull in Cave 7—those, and so many other moments, will remain imperishable in my memory. And as I think back on the Comb, another realization dawns in my head: that no matter how long I live, no matter how many more years I can hike, there will always be canyons in the Southwest down which I can set off for the first time, or cliffs and mesas yet to climb, where I will have the chance to discover ruins and rock art panels that, no matter who else may have found them before me, are like nothing else I have ever seen.

ACKNOWLEDGMENTS

OUR JOURNEY ALONG THE COMB RIDGE quite literally could not have taken place without the services of our stalwart resuppliers. We tender our heartfelt thanks not only to the punctual and reliable Jim Hook (and to his shotgun-riding sidekick, five-year-old Thomas), but to Marcia Hadenfeldt and Renée Globis as well. Marcia deserves extra credit for encouraging her husband to indulge in a monthlong truancy from his real job as co-proprietor of Far Out Expeditions—in prime guiding season, moreover. And Renée gamely took up the slack of Greg's absence during three weeks out of the first two months that their baby, Ariann, spent in this world.

Ramon Redhouse, the Navajo guide whom we hired to help us lay vital water caches, was invaluable as an intermediary with the traditional Navajos on the reservation. Among those settlers, we thank Chester and Rena Benally, as well as Mr. Parrish (whose first name we never caught), for allowing our intrusions into their backyards. And speaking of traditional Navajos, we beg Maxie Platt's forgiveness for getting between his sheep and the spring he was leading them to, for setting his dogs off on a pandemonium of barking, and (perhaps) for startling and bewildering the man himself with our strange advent in his homeland.

Winston Hurst, with his own lifelong acquaintance with and love of the Comb Ridge as well as his professional acumen as an archaeologist, served us as a wry and savvy consultant. The keenest student to date of the Navajo history and cosmogony of the region, Robert S. McPherson, likewise deepened our understanding of the landscape we traversed, chiefly through the pages of his excellent books.

At the Mountaineers Books, Cassandra Conyers, Don Graydon, Laura Drury, Alice Tew, and Joeth Zucco skillfully shepherded our "project" through its transformation into a veritable book. My agent, Stuart Krichevsky, and his two crackerjack assistants, Shana Cohen and Liz Coen, played critical roles in similarly transmuting a long, hard walk into a pictorial narrative.

The North Face very generously supplied the three of us with all the latest high-tech, super-lightweight gear we could possibly have desired to ease the logistical doldrums of a 125-mile backpack. At that company, Katie Ramage efficiently handled our requests and got the stuff to us in plenty of time. Jeff Bowman likewise outfitted us with invaluable equipment from MSR and Therm-a-Rest. And Sabine Meyer, photo editor of *National Geographic Adventure*, supplied Greg with more free film than he could possibly shoot in eighteen days— and free processing to boot.

Finally, to all the folks—friends, relatives, editors, clients, and the like—whom we inconvenienced by going in absentia during September 2004, we offer our gratitude for cutting us enough slack so that we could pursue a lark that was dear to our hearts.

SELECTED
BIBLIOGRAPHY

Aton, James M., and Robert S. McPherson. *River Flowing from the Sunrise: An Environmental History of the Lower San Juan.* Logan, Utah: 2000.

Blackburn, Fred, and Ray A. Williamson. *Cowboys & Cave Dwellers: Basketmaker Archaeology in Utah's Grand Gulch.* Santa Fe: 1997.

Gillmor, Frances, and Louisa Wade Wetherill. *Traders to the Navajos: The Wetherills of Kayenta.* Albuquerque: 1934.

Gregory, Herbert E. *The Navajo Country: A Geographic and Hydrographic Reconnaissance of Parts of Arizona, New Mexico, and Utah.* Washington, DC: 1916.

Gregory, Herbert E. *The San Juan Country: A Geographic and Geologic Reconnaissance of Southeastern Utah.* Washington, DC: 1938.

Haas, Jonathan, and Winifred Creamer. *Stress and Warfare among the Kayenta Anasazi of the Thirteenth Century A. D.* Chicago: 1993.

Holiday, John, and Robert S. McPherson. *A Navajo Legacy: The Life and Teachings of John Holiday.* Norman, Oklahoma: 2005.

Hurst, Winston B., and Christy G. Turner II. "Rediscovering the 'Great Discovery': Wetherill's First Cave 7 and Its Record of Basketmaker Violence." In *Anasazi Basketmaker: Papers from the 1990 Wetherill–Grand Gulch Symposium.* Edited by V. M. Atkins. Salt Lake City: 1993.

Kerasote, Ted. *Out There: In the Wild in a Wired Age.* Stillwater, Minnesota: 2004.

McNitt, Frank. *Richard Wetherill: Anasazi.* Albuquerque: 1957.

McPherson, Robert S. "Posey War." In *Utah History Encyclopedia.* *www.media.utah.edu/UHE/p/POSEYWAR.html.*

McPherson, Robert S. *Sacred Land, Sacred View: Navajo Perceptions of the Four Corners Region.* Provo, Utah: 1992.

McPherson, Robert S. *The Journey of Navajo Oshley: An Autobiography and Life History.* Logan, Utah: 2000.

Macomb, J. N. *Report of the Exploring Expedition from Santa Fé, New Mexico, to the Junction of the Grand and Green Rivers of the Great Colorado of the West, in 1859.* Washington, DC: 1876.

Miller, David E. *Hole-in-the-Rock: An Epic in the Colonization of the*

Great American West. Salt Lake City: 1959.

Moorehead, Warren K., and Lewis W. Gunkel. "In Search of a Lost Race." In the *Illustrated American*, eleven issues between May 28, 1892, and August 13, 1892.

Morris, Tonya. "Posey: A Leader of the Witapunuche Utes." *www. sanjuan.k12.ut.us/sjsample/POSEY/Posey4.htm.*

Roberts, David. *In Search of the Old Ones: Exploring the Anasazi World of the Southwest.* New York: 1996.

Topping, Gary. *Glen Canyon and the San Juan Country.* Moscow, Idaho: 1997.

Wetherill, Benjamin Alfred. *The Wetherills of Mesa Verde: Autobiography of Benjamin Alfred Wetherill.* Edited by Maurine S. Fletcher. Lincoln, Nebraska: 1977.

GLOSSARY

Anasazi. Archaeological designation for the ancestors of today's Pueblo Indians, who flourished across much of the Colorado Plateau for thousands of years before the abandonment of the northern part of that homeland just before AD 1300.

arête. A steep ridge on a peak or a pinnacle.

arroyo. An erosion-gouged ravine, usually dry.

Athapaskans. A classification of various Native American tribes originating in subarctic Canada. In the Southwest, the only Athapaskans are the Navajos and the Apaches.

atlatl. A spear-thrower, made of a throwing stick and a dart with a **chert** projectile point, launched with a javelin-like motion. Both for hunting and for warfare, the atlatl preceded the invention of the bow and arrow.

Basketmaker. The phase of Anasazi culture roughly between 1200 BC and AD 750. So named for the exquisitely wrought baskets that preceded the invention of pottery.

bivouac. To spend the night out without a tent or (usually) a sleeping bag.

chert. The kind of igneous rock from which Native Americans fashioned points and tools.

cist. A small storage bin, usually made of upright sandstone slabs, found inside a cave or alcove.

col. A pass or gap between two mountains or ridge crests.

Diné. The Navajos' name for themselves; also, the Navajo language.

Dinétah. The Navajo homeland in northwestern New Mexico, where the people flourished from about AD 1600 to 1775.

draw. A shallow valley.

escarpment. A long, continuous cliff.

fin. A slender ridge or **arête** (q. v.).

gendarme. A tower or pinnacle of rock.

hogan. The traditional Navajo dwelling.

hoodoo. A mushroom-shaped pinnacle of rock, usually protruding from a ridgeline.

kachina. Any of about 400 semi-supernatural beings, believed by the Pueblo Indians to ensure rain and fertility.

Kachina Phenomenon. The religion, based on **kachinas** (q. v.), that has anchored Puebloan society from about AD 1325 to the present.

kiva. An underground chamber in an Anasazi site, usually round, sometimes (though not definitively) thought to be reserved for ceremonial use.

lithic. Having to do with stone. A **lithic scatter** is an assemblage of chert flakes lying on the ground, the debris left from toolmaking.

loophole/porthole. A small, round tube or aperture in the wall of an Anasazi dwelling, probably used to spy on unwelcome intruders.

mano. A stone used to grind corn, seeds, and nuts. See **metate**.

massif. A range of mountains or cliffs.

metate. The stone basin on which corn, seeds, and nuts are ground with a **mano**.

midden. The trash dump just below a prehistoric site, usually rich in cultural debris.

monocline. A stratigraphic thrust in the earth's crust along a single direction, usually caused by a unique geological upheaval.

Numic. A classification for Native American tribes including Utes, Shoshone, and Paiutes.

olla. A large ceramic water jug.

petroglyph. A rock art figure created by carving into the surface of a cliff or boulder.

pictograph. A rock art figure created by painting on a cliff or boulder.

potsherd. A broken piece of any ceramic vessel. Also **sherd**.

prong. A small upthrusting point of rock.

roomblock. A dwelling (usually Anasazi) that consists of two or more rooms sharing common walls.

slickrock. Generic term for smooth, undulating sandstone canyon walls.

tablita. An crescent-shaped Anasazi headdress.

talus. Jumbled fields or piles of stones.

tamarisk. A nasty bush, not indigenous to the Southwest, that flourishes along watercourses.

tank. A natural pothole that holds water after rainfall.

Tusayan. Pertaining to the Kayenta Anasazi who flourished in northeastern Arizona.

wash. A canyon or ravine, often dry, usually shallow.

INDEX

Navajo Indians
arrival in Four Corners, 58–59, 114–116
culture of
animal omens, 21
breaking the ice with strangers, 22–23
definitions for rain, 39, 167
isolation, 57
languages spoken by, 28
names for rock formations, 21, 58, 160
perceptions about Comb Ridge, 58–61
rock art, 25–29, 73–74
taboos about death, 28
views toward Anasazi, 29–32, 61, 114, 116, 150
Long Walk, 58, 113
Navajo Mountain, 59, 112–113, 162–163
Navajo Nation, 101
Navajo Reservation, 15–16, 18, 29–31, 37–38, 162, 164–165
Nelson, Nels, 170
Newberry, John S., 14–15
Nielson, Jens, 133
Nokaito Bench, 107
North Whiskers Draw, 166–167, 173, 176
Numic peoples, 93, 184

Old Dugway, 154, 159
Old Ones (Anasazi), 31–32, 114, 116, 120, 166
Oljato, 112–113
Oshley, Navajo, 59–61
Out There: In the Wild in a Wired Range (Kerasote book), 65
Outside (magazine), 44, 104
Over the Edge (Child book), 44
Owl Canyon, 131

Paiute Indians, 162–164
Palisades, 16
Paonia, 102
Parrish, Mr., 19–21, 23–24
Pecos Conference, 83, 170
Pecos Pueblo, 83
Perfect Kiva ruins, 51
Perkins, Hyrum, 133
petroglyphs, 27–29, 31, 84, 97, 106, 114, 122, 142–143, 146, 184
pictographs, 10–11, 27, 31, 84, 89–91, 114, 121–122, 142–143, 184
Place of Moonlight Water, 112–113
Platt, Maxie, 98–99, 136
plazas, 94
Posey, 163–164

Posey's Trail, 161
Posey's War, 161–164
Postcards from the Ledge (Child book), 42, 44
potholes, 18, 64, 67–70, 79, 139, 158, 184
pothunting, 155–156
potsherds, 64, 82, 146, 154–155, 184
pottery, 146–147
Pottery Shrine, 154
Princess (mummy), 172
Procession Panel, 139–143
Prudden, T. Mitchell, 156–157
Pueblo I, 83, 161
Pueblo II, 83
Pueblo III, 83–84, 86, 106, 120, 145, 161, 174
Pueblo Indians, 10, 30–32, 37, 92–93, 95, 114–115, 143
Pueblo IV, 83
Puebloans. *See* Pueblo Indians
pueblos, 30
push-pull theory, 93–94

Rainbow Plateau, 66
Recapture Creek, 14, 155
Recapture Lodge, 32, 66, 176
Red Lake, 113
Redd, Charles, 132
Redhouse, Ramon, 19–20, 23, 41, 57–58, 68
"Rediscovering the 'Great Discovery': Wetherill's First Cave 7 and its Record of Basketmaker Violence" (Hurst and Turner article), 174
reverse archaeology, 172, 174
Richard Wetherill: Anasazi (McNitt book), 171
Rio Grande River, 93–94
Road Canyon, 132
Roberts, David
career of, 50–51
climbing experience, 50–51
encounters with the Navajo, 66–67, 98–99
interest in Anasazi culture, 45–46, 51, 58
pictures of, 111, 124
relationships
with Child, 42, 44–46, 51–56
with Hadenfeldt, 45–46, 49–56
Roberts, Jenny, 104–105, 166
Rock and Ice (magazine), 44
rock art
by Anasazi, 10–11, 37, 73, 84–85, 89–91, 97, 106, 121–122, 141–143
by Navajo, 25–29, 73–74

ABOUT THE AUTHORS

David Roberts is the author of seventeen books, including, most recently, *On the Ridge between Life and Death: A Climbing Life Reexamined*, as well as two collections of adventure essays, *Moments of Doubt* and *Escape Routes*, published by The Mountaineers Books. During the 1960s and 1970s, he led or co-led thirteen expeditions to the mountains of Alaska and the Yukon, making many first ascents. He lives in Cambridge, Massachusetts.

Greg Child is one of the preeminent mountaineers of his generation, with ascents of K2, Everest, Gasherbrum IV, Shivling, and other high and dangerous peaks to his credit, as well as numerous new routes on mountains and crags all over the world. He is the author of six books, including *Over the Edge: The True Story of Four American Climbers' Kidnap and Escape in the Mountains of Central Asia*, as well as *Mixed Emotions*, *Postcards from the Ledge*, and *Thin Air: Encounters in the Himalayas*, published by The Mountaineers Books. A native of Australia, he lives in Castle Valley, Utah.

THE MOUNTAINEERS, founded in 1906, is a nonprofit outdoor activity and conservation club, whose mission is "to explore, study, preserve, and enjoy the natural beauty of the outdoors. . . . " Based in Seattle, Washington, the club is now the third-largest such organization in the United States, with seven branches throughout Washington State.

The Mountaineers sponsors both classes and year-round outdoor activities in the Pacific Northwest, which include hiking, mountain climbing, ski-touring, snowshoeing, bicycling, camping, kayaking, nature study, sailing, and adventure travel. The club's conservation division supports environmental causes through educational activities, sponsoring legislation, and presenting informational programs.

All club activities are led by skilled, experienced instructors, who are dedicated to promoting safe and responsible enjoyment and preservation of the outdoors.

If you would like to participate in these organized outdoor activities or the club's programs, consider a membership in The Mountaineers. For information and an application, write or call The Mountaineers, Club Headquarters, 300 Third Avenue West, Seattle, WA 98119; 206-284-6310. You can also visit the club's website at www.mountaineers.org or contact The Mountaineers via email at clubmail@mountaineers.org.

The Mountaineers Books, an active, nonprofit publishing program of the club, produces guidebooks, instructional texts, historical works, natural history guides, and works on environmental conservation. All books produced by The Mountaineers Books fulfill the club's mission.

Send or call for our catalog of more than 500 outdoor titles:

The Mountaineers Books
1001 SW Klickitat Way, Suite 201
Seattle, WA 98134
800-553-4453
mbooks@mountaineersbooks.org
www.mountaineersbooks.org

The Mountaineers Books is proud to be a corporate sponsor of The Leave No Trace Center for Outdoor Ethics, whose mission is to promote and inspire responsible outdoor recreation through education, research, and partnerships. The Leave No Trace program is focused specifically on human-powered (nonmotorized) recreation.

Leave No Trace strives to educate visitors about the nature of their recreational impacts, as well as offer techniques to prevent and minimize such impacts. Leave No Trace is best understood as an educational and ethical program, not as a set of rules and regulations.

For more information, visit *www.LNT.org*, or call 800-332-4100.

OTHER TITLES YOU MIGHT ENJOY FROM
THE MOUNTAINEERS BOOKS

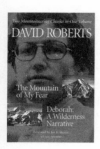

**David Roberts: The Mountain of My Fear;
Deborah: A Wilderness Narrative**
David Roberts
Two of Roberts' best-loved works collected into one volume.

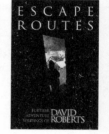

**Escape Routes:
Further Adventure Writings of
David Roberts**
David Roberts
Essays from David Roberts' travels to the
ends of the earth and back again.

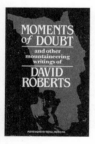

**Moments of Doubt and Other
Mountaineering Writings of David Roberts**
David Roberts
More adventure tales in these 20 essays and
articles on mountaineering and travel.

The Beckoning Silence
Joe Simpson
Brash and colorful, Simpson has
never been more entertaining.

**Postcards from the Ledge: Collected
Mountaineering Writings of Greg Child**
Greg Child
Selections of the best (often humorous)
writings from elite mountaineer Greg Child.

**Minus 148°:
First Winter Ascent of Mt. McKinley**
Art Davidson
A "best adventure book" pick by
National Geographic Adventure:
experience the tragedy and triumph
of the first winter ascent of Mt. McKinley.

Available at fine bookstores and outdoor stores, by phone at
800-553-4453 or on the web at *www.mountaineersbooks.org*

THE MOUNTAINEERS BOOKS